To David Bothewe

With best wishes
Bet Cherington

Facing the World

July 1989

Facing the World
An Anthology of Poetry
for Humanists

Chosen by

Bet Cherrington

Pemberton, London 1989

First published in 1989 by Pemberton Publishing Company, for the Rationalist Press Association, 88 Islington High Street, London N1.

ISBN 0 301 88002 6
ISBN 0 301 88001 8

Printed in Great Britain by Goodwin Press Ltd, Goodwin Street, London N4 3HQ.

ACKNOWLEDGEMENTS

I owe thanks to many people who have given me support, suggestions and criticism. Particularly, I will mention Helen Hampson, whose selection of many poems helped to set the stamp on the style and direction of this work; Marianne Leavitt, the American novelist, for her accurate criticism and her lively interest; and many relatives and friends, among them Alison Hall, Dorothy Mulelly and Leonara Murton. I want to mention the help of the following Humanists: John White, Diana Rookledge, Harold Blackham and David Oppenheimer. Jim Herrick and Nicolas Walter did me the honour of accepting the Anthology for publication and have steadfastly persevered to bring it to publication. My husband, Paul, who first suggested I should "do something about poetry" has sustained my morale and given me consistent practical help over the years. Thank you, all of you.

Bet Cherrington

MacDiarmid, Hugh (Martin Brian & O'Keefe Ltd); Masefield, John (The Society of Authors as the Literary representatives of the Estate of John Masefield); McGinley, Phyllis (Martin Secker & Warburg Ltd); Morgan, Edwin (*Poems of Thirty Years* Carcanet Press Ltd); Morton, J. B. (A.D. Peters & Co Ltd); Milne, A. A. (*Winnie-the-Pooh*, Methuen Children's books); Mitchell, Adrian (*Collected Poems 1953 - 1979* Allison & Busby Ltd); Montague, John (*A Chosen Light*, 1967 and *Selected Poems*, 1982); Nash, Ogden (*I wouldn't have missed it*, Andre Deutsch); Nicholson, Norman (David Higham Associates Ltd); Plomer, William (*Collected Poems, Jonathan Cape Ltd); Pound Ezra (Collected Shorter Poems*, Faber & Faber Ltd); Reed, Jeremy (*By the fisheries*, Jonathan Cape Ltd); Sandburg, Carl (*Cornhuskers*, 1918, Harcourt Brace Jovanich, Inc); Sassoon, Siegfried (G. T. Sassoon); Smith, Stevie (*The Collected Poems of Stevie Smith*, Penguin Modern Classics, James MacGibbon); Stephens, James (The Society of Authors on behalf of the copyright owner. Mrs Iris Wise); Thomas, Dylan (David Higham Associates Ltd); Young, Andrew (*The Poetical Works* Secker & Warburg Ltd); White T. H. (*A Joy Proposed*, Secker & Warburg Ltd).

CONTENTS

FOREWORD

And all those dreams by which men long live well
Are magic-lanterned on the smoke of hell.

WILLIAM EMPSON, here, is writing about how "dreams" of
a long and happy life are illusions only. The reality is that
all lives, to a varying extent, are filled with pain and
suffering. One of the traditional "consolations" of the
religions is that after death everything will be made all right;
the good will be rewarded and the bad punished.

We must face the fact, without knowing for certain—
because death is "the undiscover'd country from whose
bourn no traveller returns'—that this is probably not so.
The rationalist and the atheist must be stoical. There is no
afterlife, and justice may never be done. Bernard Shaw once
wrote that all great truths began as blasphemies. It's
certainly true of this one, as the persecution of unbelievers
throughout the centuries adequately proves. If we want
justice on this earth, in this life, we must get it ourselves.
"Life is a responsible art", as Bet Cherrington says in her
Preface.

Life, however, needn't be dismal. Good poems have a
vitality and a rhythmical persuasiveness that is deeply
satisfying. Happy poems have always been few, because
happiness, as has been said, "writes white"; but a problem
stated, if not a problem solved, is at least a problem on the
way to a solution. Sad poems, in fact, are satisfying too. As
religions would like to be (in the intervals between killing the
supporters of their rivals), poetry itself can be a consolation.

Poetry, too, can be of very many kinds. It extends from the
formal wisdom of Pope to Pooh Bear's simple song
"Cottleston Pie", taking in Herrick's "Gather ye rosebuds"
lyric, poems that describe the experience of women, poems
that are bitter, funny, satirical, heartbreaking. A book like
this always contains surprises. It's always good to find a
poem you've never seen before.

Every reader will have his or her likes and dislikes; that
goes without saying. But it would be an odd person who
didn't enjoy a very large number of these poems—assuming
that he or she were sensitive to verse and not in a similar
category to the tone-deaf and the colourblind.

GAVIN EWART

1

PREFACE

HUMANISM AS A PHILOSOPHY for living is as old as human thought and as widespread as the human race. A nontheistic, sceptical view has always been held by some men and women; sometimes openly, when it was safe, more often covertly, since priests decreed that unbelievers should be punished, perhaps for the good of their souls. The expression of Humanism has varied according to the society in which the Humanist lived, and to the dominant beliefs of that society. The line of descent can be traced from Confucius to Bertrand Russell, via all the civilisations which have come between. For me, and for many today in this country and at this time, Humanism could be shortly stated thus:

> This life is all we have, and between birth and death each of us should achieve the maximum enrichment of life as an individual and for the common good. Our only afterlife will be in the memory others have of us. There is no given overall purpose to life, but we can choose many purposes of our own whether alone or in a group, consecutively or simultaneously, and for next week, next year or many decades ahead.

Our circumstances vary and fluctuate continually. If our experiences delight us, we try to prolong or repeat them; if they are fairly satisfactory, we can keep our anxieties under control and live creatively. If they are unbearable, we rally our forces and our friends to change them. We never "arrive", as fresh demands are continually made on us however far we press along our chosen path.

Is it tragic that death cuts us off? It might be more tragic if we could never die, nor young life succeed us.

The Humanist virtues, as indicated in Barbara Smoker's *What's this Humanism* (1973), are intellectual integrity, tolerance, breadth of sympathy and co-operative endeavour. To this list I would add courage, self-discipline, and two traits which go together—a sense of proportion and a sense of humour.

Humanists do not think that there are any gods, but admit that there are many unsolved problems and mysteries. Our policy is to continue to live as if we were alone, unsupported by any transcendent force. This life is enough, and more; it

2

can be experienced directly through our senses, and examined in the visual arts, in music, in literature, in prose or equally discriminatingly in poetry—which brings me to this anthology.

★   ★   ★

The idea of compiling an "Anthology for Humanists" came to me when, chancing to read Marvell's Satires, I was startled to find the line "Priests were the first deluders of mankind". Marvell did not stop there, but put in a good word for Eve! For the first time I realised that verses critical of religion and of the male hierarchy, which is so essential to it, had been suppressed, and I began to look for them. "Doubt and Disbelief" became the core of my selection.

But the sceptical view soon seemed inadequate, a prelude to a more widespread examination of human life. I wanted to see how the Humanist attitude could apply to other areas of experience. I wanted to strip away confusions, to allow people to speak for themselves about their pain or joy without the intrusion of the supernatural element. These "confusions" I later put where I think they belong—in the world of fantasy.

The first section I called "The Human Condition". It was the first area of the broad Humanist attitude which occurred to me, the obvious raw material of human life: birth, marriage and death, or better, birth, growth, reproduction, development to the maximum, decline and death. I wanted to preclude value-judgments and find out how poets expressed not their views, but their experience of these major events and phases of life.

The material was available, massively; the only problem was to select and set limits. I decided to exclude translations and to include the whole range of poets, regardless of their beliefs. (So this is an anthology for Humanists, and of the Humanist perspective, but not entirely by Humanists— some of those included held sincere if unorthodox religious beliefs.) I found for the section on "The Human Condition" poets who showed what it felt like to be a child, an adolescent, a lover, a parent; what it is like to feel strength

3

in your prime, weakness in your old age; to see others die; to be ill, to work, to fight, to create works of art.

All this time a question was forming in my mind and becoming more pressing: isn't all this merely descriptive? What about action, the positive life-stance, decisions taken in dreadful dilemmas? What attitude to life should Humanists adopt, defiant or submissive, critical or complacent? At first I sought good examples. Later I came to the view that "there are two kinds of example, and one of them's a warning". I christened this section "Facing the World", and selected recommendations and stances of all kinds; exhortations and oblique suggestions for a way of life.

At this point, the Pemberton Publishing Company, which showed interest in publishing the anthology, suggested that the manuscript could be considerably expanded. At that time I felt that there was a logical progression from human experience through to examining religious views and on to the choice of attitude or cluster of attitudes to life. It was a coherent sequence not a random series of topics which could be added to or reduced without detriment to the whole. However, to enlarge the anthology would allow the insertion, within this frame, of many and various poems which I had had regretfully to discard as irrelevant.

These fell into three distinct categories. First, there were environmental poems, those in which non-human creatures and also landscapes seemed to merge with human life. Trout felt terror, birds sang "because they felt like it" (as Julian Huxley said). People and their surroundings seemed to interact and influence each other. Is there in fact an absolute border between the macrocosm of the world and the microcosm inside the human brain? Poems in this section "Humanity in Nature" are concerned with such questions and also with doubts about our survival unless we are aware and are prepared to act positively for survival.

With the extra scope of more space, I now added a section of imaginative poems which embodied enjoyment rather than earnestness. I decided, with relief, to call it "Fantasy" and set about reading in a different region. Witches, werewolves, angels and devils broke bounds and cavorted around with Mad Hatters and magic carpets in a kind of Dance of Disneyland.

Fantasy fitted into the general scheme of the anthology as it found a place for what was not specifically Humanist, but which was vividly human. How delightful to have the chance of putting in a hymn or two! To give the imagination free rein as the undifferentiated ground upon which we can erect our definitions and compartments! To rejoice in the imaginative range and brilliance of the human mind!

Finally I endeavoured to collect poems about Time. This was the hardest task, but I felt that to discuss human life without examining Time was like trying to breathe without air. Time is invisible, but absolutely necessary, and there is much still to find out about it. I am not satisfied with this section, but it is a start.

In its completed stage the anthology consisted of the six parts presented here: ''The Human Condition'', giving the raw materials of life; ''Doubt and Disbelief'', dealing with the question ''Why''; ''Time'' our inexorable ruler; ''Fantasy'', the untamed imagination which precedes and enlivens action; and "Facing the World'', showing alternative stances for decision- making. I strove to preserve the direction of the first draft, while extending the scope of the offerings.

My chief criterion in selecting these poems has been: Has it something to say and does it come across vigorously? The interesting questions of style, finish and verbal accuracy, I have not considered so important here. Beauty comes as a bonus, and is largely subjective. I have often chosen a poem to fill a gap in a sequence of thought, and have sometimes squeezed one in because I couldn't resist it.

Many of these verses are by women, speaking for themselves. The women's movement has increased both our confidence in ourselves as women and our output of poems. Half the population is female, and it is just and proper to give us adequate representation, especially as women's poetry often moves into areas of life which men prefer not to discuss.

Some famous poems are included and some quite unknown ones. All are in English and there are no translations. My aim has been to provide material covering a wide range of thought and expression, to give the reader ample choice while keeping within my chosen limits.

The movement in life from experience to reasonable decision isn't, of course, a once-for-all achievement. It is spasmodic, repeated, shirked, piecemeal, never fully and finally completed. But the anthology gives a certain guidance and offers routes to decision-making: it embodies the idea of moving towards maturity in spite of shocks, disasters, disappointments or sudden changes both for worse or better. Life is a responsible art, and the study of various responses to its demands leads to a relatively better performance—that is my hope.

May this anthology give enjoyment and show how rich and complex life is. I hope that people will be happy to read through or to dip into this book, which has given me joy in the making.

PART I

THE HUMAN CONDITION

Know then thyself, presume not God to scan;
The proper studt of mankind is man.

The whole of this Anthology is an attempt to follow this dictum of Alexander Pope, and this first part deals directly with the experience of being human. ("Man" in this context meaning human beings.) The esential human being is conceived, born, lives, loves and dies. "Presume not God to scan" is comparable to the Confucian advice "Never discuss infinity". Better to concentrate on what is and what might be.

Hardy's findings in "Heredity" have been confirmed by Crick and Watson in their genetic researches. The genes are not strictly eternal, but as long as the family line survives, so do they, although they may, like cards, be dealt round into different hands.

The sequence of poems from "The Cell' to Herrick's "Upon Prew, His Maid" cover the main physical and emotional experiences of human life, are fairly easy to understand, being straightforward descriptions of events and feelings. The remainder are about many different matters: illness, sleep, grief; Crabbe's note on the subjectivity of judgement, how it changes with mood; several poems on the important areas of work and war; and of the experience of the creative artist. Browning's brilliant portrait of the Duke in "My Last Duchess" shows the callousness in human relationships of the discriminating art collector out to possess priceless objects. Dylan Thomas's "In my craft or sullen art" expresses a poet's feeling for humanity and his disregard for money-making. Taken as a whole, these poems are descriptive rather than judgmental.

Know then thyself. . .

KNOW then thyself, presume not God to scan;
The proper study of mankind is man.
Placed on this isthmus of a middle state,
A being darkly wise, and rudely great:
With too much knowledge for the sceptic side,
With too much weakness for the stoic's pride,
He hangs between; in doubt to act, or rest,
In doubt to deem himself a god, or beast;
In doubt his mind or body to prefer,
Born but to die, and reasoning but to err
Alike in ignorance, his reason such,
Whether he thinks too little, or too much:
Chaos of thought and passion, all confused;
Still by himself abused, or disabused;
Created half to rise, and half to fall;
Great lord of all things, yet a prey to all;
Sole judge of truth, in endless error hurled:
The glory, jest and riddle of the world!

From *Essay on Man*

ALEXANDER POPE
(1688-1744)

Heredity

I AM the family face;
Flesh perishes, I live on,
Projecting trait and trace
Through time to times anon,
And leaping from place to place
Over oblivion.

The years-heired feature that can
In curve and voice and eye
Despise the human span
Of durance—that is I;
The eternal thing in man,
That heeds no call to die.

THOMAS HARDY
(1840-1928)

'The Cell Lay Inside Her Body'

THE cell lay inside her body
(calm as my arm now lies
between her legs).
The cell grew. It divided.
Went on dividing—clunk!
Twist and twist again the helix flipped
and—clunk!
And twist again—clunk! Bravo!
Until it was all happening on all sides

at all times
(like a plant growing at night)
like a great factory
pounding and hissing and turning corners,
pushing out new seaweed shapes
like hands and ears and feet
turning human . . . .

Yet she slept. Yet she walked,
through the day. Like a slow plant.
Pretending it wasn't happening,
this cracking of mountains,
this breaking of stone,
this multiplication of the five loaves
and still there was more
and still there was more—
five thousand thousand million cells.

And now, here he is!
He weeps, he cries, he laughs,
he gives all manner of signs of life—
what a colourful wind-kicking rag he is!

A kite who lunges at the sky.
And his dark plant-time
is slipping out of sight
through the closing fontanelle.

I stand to him as the slow plants stand to me—
tender and attender, watcher and blesser.
We breathe exchanges.
I give him my face.   He gives me his smile.
I give him my hand.   He bites it.

from *A Patching Together*

MURRAY EDMOND
(1949-   )

*To My Children Unknown, Produced By
Artificial Insemination*

TO MY children unknown:
Space projects,
My galactic explosions—
I do not even know
How many of you there are,
If ever you got off the launching pad.

All I know is,
As a "donor"
I received acknowledgement of
"The success of the experiment".
All boys.
Mission completed.

I gave my all.
Under rigid scientific conditions,
In the interests of science I
Was willingly raped:
The exciting suction pump
In a stark laboratory,
Sterile,
Beneath blazing lights,
Masked assistants all eyes.

That laboratory bench
Was the only home I ever made,
My single marriage bed.
A kind of actor, I performed,
Projected my part.
All systems were go.
And come. My role,
The onlie begetter
Of these ensuing
Muppets.

All happiness! Yes—
After the initial mild embarrassment
At making an exhibition of myself
(In front of all those students!)
Despite the public nature of the occasion
And the scientific dispassion
I endured with moody willingness
The blastoff of private pleasure
That sent me to the point of no return
And even beyond,
Back to where I came from,
Into outer space.

My sample defrozen, docketed
Even before the almost endless countdown
Of detumescence.
I was advised, clinically speaking,
Not to think of "her"
As "the wife", but only as
"The recipient". The tool
Simply as "the reproductive mechanism",
My essential juices
"Prime sperm" (Caucasian.)

On to the Womb, the Moon!
Countdown to zero! Takeoff!
Rockets away! Man in space!
Into orbit! Gee, what a view!
Back to the Womb, the Moon!
To the Lake of Sleep,
The Marsh of Death,
The Sea of Showers.
The trip one long ejaculation . . . . .

Why do I never wonder who you are, wives—
You whose great bowl of a thousand wombs
Bled to a stitch in time?
Even before the nuptial night
Our divorce was final. Could I care much less
About the offspring of my loins, sprigs
Of a poet's side-job? I feel your absence
Only as I might feel amputated limbs.

At least I'm spared

                        The patter of tiny feet

Get lost,
Scions of my poetry, my poverty.
I was well paid to engender you.
(Non-taxable income from personal assets.)

Better for us never
To know a father. If only
You could never know your mother!

So be nice, be clever.
Adventurers, in setting forth
Have never a thought for your begetter.
But zoom in on that eternity
Promised by your patron, your donor,
By your ever-dying poet
Who remains
Your humble servant.

                              JAMES KIRKUP
                              (1923-   )

12

Baby Song

FROM the private ease of Mother's womb
I fall into the lighted room.

Why don't they simply put me back
Where it is warm and wet and black?

But one thing follows on another.
Things were different inside Mother.

Padded and jolly I would ride
The perfect comfort of her inside.

They tuck me in a rustling bed
—I lie there, raging, small, and red.

I may sleep soon, I may forget,
But I won't forget that I regret.

A rain of blood poured round her womb,
But all time roars outside this room.

THOM GUNN
(1929-   )

De Puero Balbutiente

METHINKS 'tis pretty sport to hear a child,
Rocking a word in mouth yet undefiled;
The tender racquet rudely plays the sound,
Which, weakly bandied, cannot back rebound;
And the soft air the softer roof doth kiss,
With a sweet dying and a pretty miss,
Which hears no answer yet from the white rank
Of teeth, not risen from their coral bank.
The alphabet is searched for letters soft,
To try a word before it can be wrought,
And when it slideth forth, it goes as nice
As when a man doth walk upon the ice.

THOMAS BASTARD
(1566-1618)

13

The Conventionalist

FOURTEEN-YEAR-OLD, why must you giggle and dote?
Fourteen-year-old, why are such a goat?
I'm fourteen years old, that is the reason,
I giggle and dote in season.

STEVIE SMITH
(1902-1971)

A Basuto Coming-of-Age

THE winter sun, a distant roar of light,
Immensely sets, and far below this place
Cold on the plains the vast blue tides of night
Press on, and darken as they race.
Out of retreat, with dancing and with dirges,
Men bring a boy in whom a man emerges.

The new man sees anew the twisted aloes,
His father's house, his cattle in the shallows,
And up the hill a crowd of girls advancing
To carry him to drinking and to dancing—
His heart leaps up as he descends the steep,
For, where the boy slept, now the man shall sleep.

WILLIAM PLOMER
(1903-1973)

Ballad

RICH as the stars and poor as a beggar
Filled with every hope, yet having none
Fever-hot yet freezing, full yet racked with hunger
Coins jingle at morning, by evening they're gone.
Friends and familiarity I left at home
Being young, filled with desires and dreams
Through highways and cities I roll like a stone
I don't know what it is, but I know how it seems.

Life knocks me over easy as a feather
And every time it happens, I won't be shown.
When the day is calm, I long for stormy weather;
When winds whistle, I want them to stop blowing.
For my road is straight when I want it to turn
The grass is brown when it should be green
When I try my best, I just get burned
For I don't know what it is, just how it seems.

It seems I walked from hell to heaven
On every side, beautiful flowers were growing
Sunlight glistened on a jaybird's feather
On a hill your castle stands alone.
I stood there gaping ad moaning
Love and jealousy torn between
Said "It could be I know where I'm going
But I don't know what is, just how it seems."

Friend, since we're made of flesh and bone,
Without a risk, no one can win.
But of the ways of man and woman
I don't know what is, just how it seems.

CLARE CHERRINGTON
(1946-   )

First Love

I NE'ER was struck before that hour
  With love so sudden and so sweet.
Her face it bloomed like a sweet flower
  And stole my heart away complete.
My face turned pale as deadly pale,
  My legs refused to walk away,
And when she looked "what could I ail?"
  My life and all seemed turned to clay.

And then my blood rushed to my face
  And took my sight away.
The trees and bushes round the place
  Seemed midnight at noonday.
I could not see a single thing,
  Words from my eyes did start;
They spoke as chords do from the string
  And blood burnt round my heart.

Are flowers the winter's choice?
  Is love's bed always snow?
She seemed to hear my silent voice
  And love's appeal to know.
I never saw so sweet a face
  As that I stood before:
My heart has left its dwelling place
  And can return no more.

JOHN CLARE
(1793-1864)

A Birthday

MY heart is like a singing bird
  Whose nest is in a watered shoot;
My heart is like an apple-tree
  Whose boughs are bent with thick-set fruit;
My heart is like a rainbow shell
  That paddles in a halcyon sea;
My heart is gladder than all these
  Because my love is come to me.

Raise me a dais of silk and down;
    Hang it with vair and purple dyes;
Carve it in doves, and pomegranates,
    And peacocks with a hundred eyes;
Work it in gold and silver grapes,
    In leaves, and silver fleur-de-lys;
Because the birthday of my life
    Is come, my love is come to me.

CHRISTINA ROSSETTI
(1830-1894)

Song

TELL me where is Fancy bred,
Or in the heart or in the head?
How begot, how nourishèd?
    Reply, reply.
It is engender'd in the eyes,
With gazing fed; and Fancy dies
In the cradle where it lies.
    Let us all ring Fancy's knell:
    I'll begin it.—Ding, dong, bell!
    All: Ding, dong, bell!

(from *The Merchant of Venice*)
WILLIAM SHAKESPEARE
(1564-1616)

It is the Soul

IT is the Soul that sees; the outward eyes
Present the object, but the mind describes;
And thence delight, disgust, or cool indiff'rence rise:
When minds are joyful, then we look around,
And what is seen is all on fairy ground;
Again they sicken, and on every view
Cast their own dull and melancholy hue;
Or, if absorbed by their peculiar cares,
The vacant eye on viewless matter glares,
Our feelings still upon our views attend,
And their own natures to the objects lend;
Sorrow and joy are in their influence sure,
Long as the passion reigns th' effects endure;
But Love in minds his various changes makes,
And clothes each object with the change he takes;
His light and shade on every view he throws,
And on each object, what he feels, bestows.

from: *The Lover's Journey.*
GEORGE CRABBE
(1754-1832)

Fain Would I Change

FAIN would I change that note
To which fond love hath charm'd me
Long, long to sing by rote,
Fancying that that harm'd me:
Yet when this thought doth come,
"Love is the perfect sum
    Of all delight,"
I have no other choice
Either for pen or voice
    To sing or write.

O love! they wrong thee much
That say thy sweet is bitter,
When thy rich fruit is such
As nothing can be sweeter.
Fair house of joy and bliss
Where truest pleasure is,
  I do adore thee:
I know thee what thou art,
I serve thee with my heart,
  And fall before thee.

from *A Book of Ayres 1605*
TOBIAS HUME
(d. 1645)

The Extasie

WHERE, like a pillow on a bed,
  A pregnant banke swel'd up, to rest
The violets reclining head,
  Sat we two, one anothers best.
Our hands were firmely cimented
  With a fast balme, which thence did spring,
Our eye-beames twisted, and did thred
  Our eyes, upon one double string;
So to'entergraft our hands, as yet
  Was all the meanes to make us one,
And pictures in our eyes to get
  Was all our propagation.
As 'twixt two equall Armies, Fate
  Suspends uncertaine victorie,
Our soules, (which to advance their state,
  Were gone out,) hung 'twixt her, and mee.
And whil'st our soules negotiate there,
  Wee like sepulchrall statues lay;
All day, the same our postures were,
  And wee said nothing, all the day.

If any, so by love refin'd,
    That he soules language understood,
And by good love were grown all minde,
    Within convenient distance stood,
He (though he knew not which soul spake,
    Because both meant, both spake the same)
Might thence a new concoction take,
    And part farre purer than he came.
This Extasie doth underperplex
    (We said) and tell us what we love,
Wee see by this, it was not sexe,
    Wee see, we saw not what did move:
But as all severall soules containe
    Mixture of things, they know not what,
Love, these mixt soules, doth mixe again,
    And makes both one, each this and that.
A single violet transplant,
    The strength, the colour, and the size,
(All which before was poore, and scant,)
    Redoubles still, and multiplies.
When love, with one another so
    Interinanimates two soules,
That abler soule, which thence doth flow,
    Defects of loneliness controules.
Wee then, who are this new soule, know,
    Of what we are compos'd, and made,
For, th'Atomies of which we grow,
    Are soules, whom no change can invade.
But O alas, so long, so farre
    Our bodies why doe wee forbeare?
They are ours, though they are not wee, Wee are
    The intelligences, they the spheares.
We owe them thankes, because they thus,
    Did us, to us, at first convay,
Yeelded their forces, sense, to us,
    Nor are drosse to us, but allay.
On man heavens influence workes not so,
    But that it first imprints the ayre,
Soe soule into the soule may flow,
    Though it to body first repaire.

As our blood labours to beget
   Spirits, as like soules as it can,
Because such fingers need to knit
   That subtile knot, which makes us man:
So must pure lovers soules descend
   T'affections, and to faculties,
Which sense may reach and apprehend,
   Else a great Prince in prison lies.
To'our bodies turne wee then, that so
   Weake men on love reveal'd may looke;
Loves mysteries in soules doe grow,
   But yet the body is his booke.
And if some lover, such as wee,
   Have heard this dialogue of one,
Let him still marke us, he shall see
   Small change, when we'are to bodies gone.

JOHN DONNE
(1572-1631)

By Loch Etive

THE flowers of the flags
Are like yellow birds, hanging
Over the secret pool.

The fronds of the ferns
Are like green serpents, curling
Beside the silent path.

The lashes of your lids
Are like a bird's wing, sweeping
Across your regard.

The softness of your speech
Is like rain, falling
Among parched thoughts.

The lenience of your lips
Is like a cloud, dissolving
At the kiss of the wind.

From your deep consideration
Runs the dark stream, nourishing
The lake of my delight.

BRYAN GUINNESS
(1905-   )

A Letter to Daphnis

THIS to the crown and blessing of my life,
The much loved husband of a happy wife;
To him whose constant passion found the art
To win a stubborn and ungrateful heart,
And to the world by tenderest proof discovers
They err, who say that husbands can't be lovers.
With such return of passion, as is due,
Daphnis I love, Daphnis my thoughts pursue;
Daphnis my hopes, and joys are bounded all in
       you.
Even I, for Daphnis and my promise sake,
What I in women censure, undertake.
But this from love, not vanity, proceeds;
You know who writes, and I who 'tis, that reads.
Judge not my passion by my want of skill:
Many love well, though they express it ill;
And I your censure could with pleasure bear,
Would you but soon return, and speak it here.

ANNE, COUNTESS OF WINCHELSEA
(1661-1720)

To . . .

WHEN I loved you, I can't but allow
    I had many an exquisite minute;
But the scorn that I feel for you now
    Hath even more luxury in it!

Thus, whether we're on or we're off,
    Some witchery seems to await you;
To love you is pleasant enough,
    But oh! 'tis delicious to hate you!

THOMAS MOORE
(1779-1852)

People Will Say We're in Love

But seriously, as the marriage wears on, thanks for the memory of hauling prams and shopping up icy door-
steps, equally as for the kisses and the dem-
onstrative eyes. Wives work hard. Cathy and her moor-
land romance are fine in the mind, but the car-
ing for babies is the real and most test-
ing fact of a union. The children are the shar-
ing. It's always Housewives v. The Rest.

And it's always into big offices for the good provid-
ers, the traditional way to keep the bank man-
agers happy. Families don't like outsid-
ers. This is men's washing and ironing, fan-
ning up a little flame of money in the current acc-
ount. Chores of the typewriter. Essential reading about Management. Not the true sweetness, sacc-
harine at best - a businessman's creed.

So the success of a marriage can be seen in the children and, believe me, certainly yours is the cred-
it, after the nappies, the orange juice, the pil-
fered hours of sleep they took from you, bed-
time too often a night shift, and loving not the novelist's outspoken rand-
y young sprawlers, pushing and shov-
ing, but tiredness, the offered and the taken hand.

GAVIN EWART (1916-   )

Mute Marriages

MUTE marriages:
The ten-ton block of ice
obstructing the throat, the heart,
the red filter of the liver,
the clogged life.

It is a glacier
in which frozen children swim
ground round with boulders,
pebbles, bits of stone
from other ice ages.

Here a lapis glitters,
Here a shard of bottle glass—
valuables and junk:
the history of a house
told in its garbage cans,
the history of a life
in its nightmares.

Speak the dream.
Follow the red thread
of the images.
Defrost the glacier
with the live heat
of your breath,
propelled by the heart's
explosion.

ERICA JONG
(1942-   )

A Farewell

WITH all my will, but much against my heart,
We two now part.
My Very Dear,
Our solace is, the sad road lies so clear.
It needs no art,
With faint, averted feet
And many a tear,
In our opposed paths to persevere.
Go thou to East, I West.
We will not say
There's any hope, it is so far away.
But, O, my best,
When the one darling of our widowhead,
The nursling Grief,
Is dead,
And no dews blur our eyes
To see the peach-bloom come in evening skies,
Perchance we may,
Where now this night is day,
And even through faith of still averted feet,
Making full circle of our banishment,
Amazed meet;
The bitter journey to the bourne so sweet
Seasoning the termless feast of our content
With tears of recognition never dry.

COVENTRY PATMORE
(1823-1896)

The Ruined Maid

"O 'MELIA, my dear, this does everything crown!
Who could have supposed I should meet you in Town?
And whence such fair garments, such prosperi-ty?"—
"O didn't you know I'd been ruined?" said she.

—'You left us in tatters, without shoes or socks,
Tired of digging potatoes, and spudding up docks;
And now you've gay bracelets and bright feathers
                                        three!'—
"Yes: that's how we dress when we're ruined," said
she.

—'At home in the barton you said "thee" and
"thou",
And "thik oon", and "theäs oon", and "t'other"; but
                                        now
Your talking quite fits 'ee for high compa-ny!" -
"A polish is gained with one's ruin," said she.

—'Your hands were like paws then, your face blue and
                                        bleak
But now I'm bewitched by your delicate cheek,
And your little gloves fit as on any la-dy!'—
"We never do work when we're ruined," said she.

—'You used to call home-life a hag-ridden dream,
And you'd sigh, and you'd sock; but at present you
                                        seem
To know not of megrims or melancho-ly!''
"True. One's pretty lively when ruined," said she.

—'I wish I had feathers, a fine sweeping gown,
And a delicate face, and could strut about Town!"—
"My dear—a raw country girl, such as you be,
Cannot quite expect that. You ain't ruined," said she.

THOMAS HARDY
(1840-1928)

Anne Donne Breaks Her Silence

I'VE held my tongue, dear John, quite long enough
And let you love your creeping tomcat way;
My voice too soft to chide your fancied gout,
Your five grey hairs—when did you last count mine?
Summer's grace was short. Mine is a drear autumnal.
Every day's St. Lucy's Day this year.

I was brought up gentle, John, and now
Passed in your paper songs from hand to hand
I am undressed in taverns, loved at one remove,
Even my fleabites licked by drunkards' tongues.
Your Kingdom, safest when with one man manned?
Hostile heathen leer across my borders.

"Come, madam, come!" Oh, no John, never again.
With twelve children I have filled our cradle;
The rocker's worn thin as a baby's rib.
It clacks upon the floor like idle wit.
I crave that rest your powers cannot defy.
I dream of Seven Sleepers in their den.

No, not for weariness of you, but chiefly
Of myself, mildly I slip away
Before you come, unrulier than the Sun.
I lean my note against the pomander.
"Your dinner's on the spit. I'm riding westward
to set your table ready—Go with God."

JANE TOZER

Remembrance

COLD in the earth—and the deep snow piled above thee,
Far, far removed, cold in the dreary grave!
Have I forgot, my only Love, to love thee,
Severed at last by Time's all-severing wave?

Now, when alone, do my thoughts no longer hover
Over the mountains, on that northern shore,
Resting their wings where heath and fern-leaves cover
Thy noble heart for ever, ever more?

Cold in the earth—and fifteen wild Decembers
From these brown hills have melted into spring—
Faithful indeed is the spirit that remembers
After such years of change and suffering!

Sweet Love of youth, forgive if I forget thee
While the World's tide is bearing me along:
Sterner desires and darker hopes beset me,
Hopes which obscure, but cannot do thee wrong!

No later light has lightened up my heaven;
No second morn has ever shone for me:
All my life's bliss from thy dear life was given—
All my life's bliss is in the grave with thee.

But, when the days of golden dreams had perished,
And even Despair was powerless to destroy,
Then did I learn how existence could be cherished,
Strengthened and fed without the aid of joy.

Then did I check the tears of useless passion,
Weaned my young soul from the yearning after thine;
Sternly denied its burning wish to hasten
Down to that tomb already more than mine!

And, even yet, I dare not let it languish,
Dare not indulge in Memory's rapturous pain;
Once drinking deep of that divinest anguish,
How could I seek the empty world again?

EMILY BRONTË
(1818-1848)

Now Fades the Last Long Streak of snow

CXV

Now fades the last long streak of snow,
  Now burgeons every maze of quick
  About the flowering squares, and thick
By ashen roots the violets blow.

Now rings the woodland loud and long,
  The distance takes a lovelier hue,
  And drowned in yonder living blue
The lark becomes a sightless song.

Now dance the lights on lawn and lea,
  The flocks are whiter down the vale,
  And milkier every milky sail
On winding stream or distant sea;

Where now the seamew pipes, or dives
  In yonder greening gleam, and fly
  The happy birds, that change their sky
To build and brood; that live their lives

From land to land; and in my breast
  Spring wakens too; and my regret
  Becomes an April violet,
And buds and blossoms like the rest.

from *In Memoriam*
ALFRED, LORD TENNYSON
(1809-1892)

Old Men

PEOPLE expect old men to die,
They do not really mourn old men.
Old men are different. People look
At them with eyes that wonder when . . .
People watch with unshocked eyes;
But old men know when an old man dies.

OGDEN NASH
(1902-1971)

Upon Prew, His Maid

IN this little urn is laid
Prudence Baldwin, once my maid,
From whose happy spark here let
Spring the purple violet.

ROBERT HERRICK
(1591-1674)

Surgery Appointment

I CAME to him lightly,
Carrying my head,
And dancing, tossed it
To his desk. He caught it well enough,
Smiling back at me.
Without a doubt
He took it for a balloon.

I came to him lightly,
My head in a paper bag.
It was a gift he accepted temporarily,
And returned with good manners.
He could not have used it.

I came to him lightly,
Lest I should trouble him,
Uncovered my severed head,
But only for a moment,
Lest that should disturb him.

I put answers to him,
Lest he be embarrassed.
He took up my line quite skilfully,
And passing the thing back,
Remarked as I had mentioned—
"You must learn to live with it.
Live in a rut. Should you have any problems,
Sort them out. Of course."

I came to him lightly
And left him the same,
My head on a string.
A cold breeze caught it,
And crushed it to drown in the sun.

I left him lightly,
Lest he should imagine
I had needed him.

MAY IVIMY
(1912-   )

Madness

THEN this is being mad; there is no more
Imagining, Ophelias of the mind.
This girl who shouts and slobbers on the floor,
Sending us frightened to the corner, is
To all the world we know now deaf and blind
And we are merely loathsome enemies.

It is the lack of reason makes us fear,
The feeling that ourselves might be like this.
We are afraid to help her or draw near
As if she were infectious and could give
Some taint, some touch of her own fantasies,
Destroying all the things for which we live.

And, worse than this, we hate the madness too
And hate the mad one. Measured off a space
There is a world where things run calm and true—
But not for us. We have to be with her
Because our minds are also out of place
And we have carried more than we can bear.

ELIZABETH JENNINGS
(1926-   )

Attempted Suicides

WE have come back.
Do not be surprised if we blink our eyes
If we stare oddly
If we hide in corners.
It is we, not you, who should show surprise.

For everything looks strange.
Roofs are made of paper
Hands are muslin
Babies look eatable.

And where do we come from?
Where did the pills take us,
The gas,
The water left pouring?
Limbo? Hell? Mere forgetfulness?

It was a lost moment,
There were no dreams,
There was simply the beyond-endurance
And then the coming-to
To you and you and you and you.

Do not ask us,
As if we were like Lazarus,
What it was like.
We never got far enough.
Now we touch ourselves and feel strange.
We have a whole world to arrange.

ELIZABETH JENNINGS

Sleep, Death's Ally . . .

SLEEP, Death's ally, oblivion of tears,
   Silence of passions, balm of angry sore,
Suspense of loves, security of fears,
   Wrath's lenitive, heart's ease, storm's calmest shore;
Senses and souls reprieved from all cumbers,
Benumbing sense of ill with quiet slumbers.

Not such my sleep, but whisperer of dreams,
   Creating strange chimaeras, faining frights;
Of day-discourses giving fancy themes,
   To make dumb-shows with worlds of antic sights;
Casting true griefs in fancy's forging mould,
Brokenly telling tales rightly foretold.

from *St Peter's Complaint*
ROBERT SOUTHWELL
(c. 1561-1595)

On the Day

HE thanks whoever-she-is for her thoughtful
Beneficence to him, in that visitation
In the early hours of the morning on the day
He travels up to hear what the X-ray meant:
Appearing out of a carmine snowdrift and
Lustrously uncovering; then extending
Such long, quick legs around him, and pushing
Him widely awake to smile at the dawn for once.

If he remembers ruefully that no one now
Visits of their own free will, that you visit
All your dreams on yourself, still, either way,
His world comes right for a while. In the life,
As it drops to the snowing street, he knows
That either some she, or some part of himself,
Wants to will him even yet into life again.
Something is pushing schemes for winning time.

ALAN BROWNJOHN
(1931-   )

The Woodspurge

THE wind flapped loose, the wind was still,
Shaken out dead from tree and hill:
I had walked on at the wind's will,—
I sat now, for the wind was still.

Between my knees my forehead was,—
My lips, drawn in, said not Alas!
My hair was over in the grass,
My naked ears heard the day pass.

My eyes, wide open, had the run
Of some ten weeds to fix upon;
Among those few, out of the sun,
The woodspurge flowered, three cups in one.

From perfect grief there need not be
Wisdom or even memory:
One thing then learnt remains to me,—
The woodspurge has a cup of three.

DANTE GABRIEL ROSSETTI
(1828-1882)

Oddments, Inklings, Omens, Moments

ODDMENTS, as when
you see through skin,
when flowers appear
to be eavesdropping,
or music somewhere
declares your mood:
when sleep fulfils
a feel of dying
or fear makes ghosts
of clothes on a chair.

Inklings, as when
some room rhymes
with a lost time,
or a book reads
like a well-known dream:
when a smell recalls
portraits, funerals,
when a wish happens
or a mirror sees
through distances.

Omens, as when
a shadow from nowhere
falls on a wall,
when a bird seems
to mimic your name,
when a cat eyes you
as though it knew
or, heavy with augury,
a crow caws
cras cras from a tree.

Moments, as when
the air's awareness
makes guesses true,
when a hand's touch
speaks past speech
or when, in poise,
two sympathies
lighten each other,
and love occurs
like song, like weather.

ALISTAIR REID

Of a Gull

OFT in my laughing rhymes I name a gull,
But this new term will many questions breed:
Therefore at first I will express at full
Who is a true and perfect gull indeed:
A gull is he who fears a velvet gown,
And when a wench is brave dares not speak to her;
A gull is he which traverseth the town,
And is for marriage known a common wooer;
A gull is he which while he proudly wears
A silver-hilted rapier by his side
Endures the lies and knocks about the ears,
Whilst in his sheath his sleeping sword doth bide;
A gull is he which wears good handsome clothes,
And stands in presence stroking up his hair,
And fills up his unperfect speech with oaths,
But speaks not one wise word throughout the year.
  But to define a gull in terms precise,
  A gull is he which seems, and is not, wise.

SIR JOHN DAVIES
(1569-1626)

Flux

THE sea is making sand out of stones,
rocks into pebbles, I am being changed.

This house is very quiet on its own,
Unruffled by adolescence which is a high tide.

The kids come in like a bore, only more often,
Leaving me later as flotsam on a bank.

I sift through the remains of each surge,
beachcombing, retrieving messages from bottles.

I am the haven for every season,
A small harbour open all year round.

Foreign travellers call in, tanned and chatty,
re-arrange themselves by the map and depart,

leaving sand in the sheets and small keepsakes,
which need dusting from time to time.

I am expected to collect all this gratefully
and model a small world of my own.

PAMELA LEWIS
(1929-   )

Teaching Keats

NERVOUSLY face them, wish I had blushful
Hippocrene to share, but drop fat grapes
of facts as they recline self-tranquillized,

having fed this morning on Midlands coal fields.
Know some of their history; try
comparisons and catch myself in unseemly

excitement at all the blood and unspent love;
return to the words, a committed fool.
Gently demand. Someone else's experience

can be your own reality if it's imagined
strongly enough, but nightingales need
as much effort as a dodo now. When they go

I lean on a desk just registering roses
in a jamjar. One is missing. Someone, simpler
than these, who communicates through Citizen's Band

with the code-name Birdman and has joined mobs
to throw stones at cars and the fuzz for fun
pulled the red petals apart this morning and ate them.

JOAN DOWNAR

She Rose

SHE rose to his requirement, dropped
The playthings of her life
To take the honourable work
Of woman and of wife,

If aught she missed in her new day
Of amplitude, or awe,
Or first perspective, or the gold
In using wore away,

It lay unmentioned, as the sea
Develops pearl and weed,
But only to himself is known
The fathoms they abide.

EMILY DICKINSON
(1830-1886)

Arm, Arm ...

ARM, arm, arm, arm, the scouts are all come in,
Keep your ranks close, and now your honours win.
Behold from yonder hill the foe appears,
Bows, bills, glaves, arrows, shields and spears,
Like a dark wood he comes, or tempest pouring;
O view the wings of horse the meadows scouring:
The vant-guard marches bravely; hark the drums—dub, dub.
    They meet, they meet, now the battle comes:
        See how the arrows fly,
        That darken all the sky.
        Hark how the trumpets sound,
        Hark how the hills rebound—tara, tara, tara.
Hark how the horses charge; in boys, in boys in—tara, tara.
    The battle totters; now the wounds begin;
        O how they cry,
        O how they die!
Room for the valiant Memnon armed with thunder,
    See how he breaks the ranks asunder.
They fly, they fly, Eumenes has the chase,
And brave Polybius makes good his place.
        To the plains, to the woods,
        To the rocks, to the floods,
They fly for succour. Follow, Follow, Follow. Hey, hey.
        Hark how the soldiers hollo!
        Brave Diocles is dead,
        And all his soldiers fled,
        The battle's won, and lost,
        That many a life hath cost.

from *The Mad Lover*
JOHN FLETCHER
(1579-1625)

Harp Song of the Dane Women

WHAT is a woman that you forsake her,
And the hearth-fire and the home-acre,
To go with the old grey Widow-maker?

She has no house to lay a guest in—
But one chill bed for all to rest in,
That the pale suns and the stray bergs nest in.

She has no strong white arms to fold you,
But the ten-times-fingering weed to hold you—
Out on the rocks where the tide has rolled you.

Yet, when the signs of summer thicken,
And the ice breaks, and the birch-buds quicken,
Yearly you turn from our side, and sicken—

Sicken again for the shouts and the slaughters.
You steal away to the lapping waters,
And look at your ship in her winter quarters.

You forget our mirth, and talk at the tables,
The kine in the shed and the horse in the stables—
To pitch her sides and go over her cables.

Then you drive out where the storm-clouds swallow,
And the sound of your oar-blades, falling hollow,
Is all we have left in the months to follow.

Ah, what is Woman that you forsake her,
And the hearth-fire and the home-acre,
To go with the old grey Widow-maker.

RUDYARD KIPLING
(1865-1936)

The Eve of Waterloo

THERE was a sound of revelry by night,
And Belgium's Capital had gathered then
Her Beauty and her Chivalry, and bright
The lamps shone o'er fair women and brave men;
A thousand hearts beat happily; and when
Music arose with its voluptuous swell,
Soft eyes looked love to eyes which spake again,
And all went merry as a marriage bell;
But hush! hark! a deep sound strikes like a rising knell!

Did ye not hear it?—No; 'twas but the wind,
Or the car rattling o'er the stony street;
On with the dance! let joy be unconfined;
No sleep till morn, when Youth and Pleasure meet
To chase the glowing Hours with flying feet—
But hark!—that heavy sound breaks in once more,
As if the clouds its echo would repeat;
And nearer, clearer, deadlier than before!
Arm! arm! it is—it is—the cannon's opening roar!

Within a windowed niche of that high hall
Sate Brunswick's fated chieftain; he did hear
That sound the first amidst the festival,
And caught its tone with Death's prophetic ear;
And when they smiled because he deemed it near,
His heart more truly knew that peal too well
Which stretch'd his father on a bloody bier,
And roused the vengeance blood alone could quell;
He rush'd into the field, and, foremost fighting, fell.

Ah! then and there was hurrying to and fro,
And gathering tears, and tremblings of distress,
And cheeks all pale, which but an hour ago
Blushed at the praise of their own loveliness;
And there were sudden partings, such as press
The life from out young hearts, and choking sighs
Which ne'er might be repeated; who could guess
If ever more should meet those mutual eyes
Since upon night so sweet such an awful morn could rise!

And there was mounting in hot haste: the steed,
The mustering squadron, and the clattering car,
Went pouring forward with impetuous speed,
And swiftly forming in the ranks of war;
And the deep thunder peal on peal afar;
And near, the beat of the alarming drum
Roused up the soldier ere the morning star;
While thronged the citizens with terror dumb,
Or whispering, with white lips—' The foe! They come!
    they come!

And wild and high the 'Cameron's Gathering' rose!
The war-note of Lochiel, which Albyn's hills
Have heard, and heard, too, have her Saxon foes:-
How in the noon of night that pibroch thrills,
Savage and shrill! But with the breath which fills
Their mountain-pipe, so fill the mountaineers
With the fierce native daring which instils
The stirring memory of a thousand years,
And Evan's, Donald's fame rings in each clansman's ears!

And Ardennes waves above them her green leaves,
Dewy with nature's tear-drops as they pass,
Grieving, if aught inanimate e'er grieves,
Over the unreturning brave,—alas!
Ere evening to be trodden like the grass
Which now beneath them, but above shall grow
In its next verdure, when this fiery mass
Of living valour, rolling on the foe
And burning with high hope, shall moulder cold and low.

Last noon beheld them full of lusty life,
Last eve in Beauty's circle proudly gay,
The midnight brought the signal-sound of strife,
The morn the marshalling in arms,—the day
Battle's magnificently stern array!
The thunder-clouds close o'er it, which when rent
The earth is covered thick with other clay,
Which her own clay shall cover, heap'd and pent,
Rider and horse,—friend, foe,—in one red burial blent!

from *Childe Harold's Pilgrimage. Canto III.*
GEORGE GORDON, LORD BYRON
(1788-1824)

The Making of a Servant

I CAN no longer ask how it feels
To be choked by a yoke-rope
Because I have seen it for myself in the chained ox.
The blindness has left my eyes. I have become aware,
I have seen the making of a servant
In the young yoke-ox.

He was sleek, lovely, born for freedom,
Not asking anything from anyone, simply
    priding himself on being a young ox.
Someone said: Let him be caught and
    trained and broken in,
Going about it as if he meant to help him.
I have seen the making of a servant
In the young yoke-ox.

He tried to resist, fighting for his freedom.
He was surrounded, fenced in with wisdom and experience.
They overcame him by trickery: "He must be trained".
A good piece of rationalisation can camouflage evil.
I have seen the making of a servant
In the young yoke-ox.

He was bound with ropes that cut into his head,
He was bullied, kicked, now and again petted,
But their aim was the same: to put a yoke on him.
Being trained in one's own interests is for the privileged.
I have seen the making of a servant
In the young yoke-ox.

The last stage. The yoke is set on him.
They tie the halter round his neck, slightly choking him.
They say the job's done, he'll be put out to work with
    the others
To obey the will of his owner and taskmaster.
I have seen the making of a servant
In the young yoke-ox.

He kicks out, trying to break away.
They speak with their whips. He turns backwards
Doing his best to resist but then they say: "Hit him".
A prisoner is a coward's plaything.
I have seen the making of a servant
In the young yoke-ox.

Though he stumbled and fell, he was bitten on the tail.
Sometimes I saw him raking at his yoke-mate
With his horns - his friend of a minute, his blood brother.
The suffering under the yoke makes for bad blood.
I have seen the making of a servant
In the young yoke-ox.

The sky seemed black as soft rain fell.
I looked at his hump, it was red,
Dripping blood, the mark of resistance.
He yearns for his home, where he was free.
I have seen the making of a servant
In the young yoke-ox.

Stockstill, tired, there was no sympathy.
He bellowed notes of bitterness.
They loosened his halter a little—to let him breathe,
They tightened it again, snatching back his breath.
I have seen the making of a servant
In the young yoke-ox.

I saw him later, broken, trained,
Pulling a double-shared plough through deep soil,
Serving, struggling for breath, in pain.
To be driven is death. Life is doing things for yourself.
I have seen the making of a servant
In the young yoke-ox.

I saw him climb the steepest roads.
He carried heavy loads, staggering —
The mud of sweat which wins profit for another.
The savour of working is a share in the harvest.
I have seen the making of a servant
In the young yoke-ox.

I saw him hungry with toil and sweat,
Eyes all tears, spirit crushed,
No longer able to resist. He was tame.
Hope lies in action aimed at freedom.
I have seen the making of a servant
In the young yoke-ox.

J. J. JOLOBE

Reconciliation

WORD over all, beautiful as the sky,
Beautiful that war and all its deeds of carnage must
    in time be utterly lost,
That the hands of the sisters Death and Night incessantly,
    softly wash agàin, and ever again, this soil'd world;
For my enemy is dead, a man divine as myself is dead.
I look where he lies white-faced and still in the coffin—
    I draw near,
Bend down and touch lightly with my lips the white face
    in the coffin.

WALT WHITMAN
(1819-1892)

Poets

IT isn't a very big cake,
some of us won't get a slice,
and that, make no mistake,
can make us not very nice
to one and all — or another
poetical sister or brother.

We all want total praise
for every word we write,
not for a singular phrase;
we're ready to turn and bite
the thick malicious reviewers,
our hated and feared pursuers.

We feel a sad neglect
when people don't buy our books;
it isn't what we expect
and gives rise to dirty looks
at a public whose addiction
is mainly romantic fiction.

We think there's something wrong
with poets that readers *read*,
disdaining our soulful song
for some pretentious creed
or poems pure and simple
as beauty's deluding dimple.

We can't imagine how
portentous nonsense by A
is loved like a sacred cow,
while dons are carried away
by B's more rustic stanzas
and C's banal bonanzas.

We have our minority view
and a sort of trust in Time;
meanwhile in this human zoo
we wander free, or rhyme,
our admirers not very many —
lucky, perhaps, to have any.

GAVIN EWART
(1916-   )

My Last Duchess

THAT'S my last Duchess painted on the wall,
Looking as if she were alive. I call
That piece a wonder, now: Frà Pandolf's hands
Worked busily a day, and there she stands.
Will't please you sit and look at her? I said
'Frà Pandolf' by design, for never read
Strangers like you that pictured countenance,
The depth and passion of its earnest glance,
But to myself they turned (since none puts by
The curtain I have drawn for you, but I)
And seemed as they would ask me, if they durst,
How such a glance came there: so, not the first
Are you to turn and ask thus. Sir, 'twas not
Her husband's presence only, called that spot
Of joy into the Duchess' cheek: perhaps
Frà Pandolf chanced to say 'Her mantle laps
Over my lady's wrist too much,' or 'Paint
Must never hope to reproduce the faint
Half-flush that dies along her throat:' such stuff
Was courtesy, she thought, and cause enough
For calling up that spot of joy. She had
A heart — how shall I say? — too soon made
    glad,

Too easily impressed; she liked whate'er
She looked on, and her looks went everywhere.
Sir, 't was all one! My favour at her breast,
The dropping of the daylight in the West,
The bough of cherries some officious fool
Broke in the orchard for her, the white mule
She rode round the terrace — all and each
Would draw from her alike the approving speech,
Or blush, at least. She thanked man, — good!
                                    but thanked
Somehow — I know not how — as if she ranked
My gift of a nine-hundred-years-old name
With anybody's gift. Who'd stoop to blame
This sort of trifling? Even had you skill
In speech —(which I have not) —to make your will
Quite clear to such an one, and say, 'Just this
Or that in you disgusts me; here you miss,
Or there exceed the mark' — and if she let
Herself be lessoned so, nor plainly set
Her wits to yours, forsooth, and made excuse,
E'en then would be some stooping; and I choose
Never to stoop. Oh sir, she smiled, no doubt,
Whene'er I passed her; but who passed without
Much the same smile? This grew; I gave commands;
Then all smiles stopped together. There she stands
As if alive. Will't please you rise? We'll meet
The company below, then. I repeat,
The Count your master's known munificence
Is ample warrant that no just pretence
Of mine for dowry will be disallowed;
Though his fair daughter's self, as I avowed
At starting, is my object. Nay, we'll go
Together down, sir. Notice Neptune, though,
Taming a sea-horse, thought a rarity,
Which Claus of Innsbruck cast in bronze for me!

ROBERT BROWNING
(1812-1889)

In my Craft or Sullen Art

IN my craft or sullen art
Excercised in the still night
When only the moon rages
And the lovers lie abed
With all their griefs in their arms,
I labour by singing light
Not for ambition or bread
Or the strut and trade of charms
On the ivory stages
But for the common wages
Of their most secret heart.

Not for the proud man apart
From the raging moon I write
On these spindrift pages
Nor for the towering dead
With their nightingales and psalms
But for the lovers, their arms
Round the griefs of the ages,
Who pay no praise or wages
Nor heed my craft or art.

DYLAN THOMAS
(1914-1953)

PART II

DOUBT AND DISBELIEF

HERE IS the chance for the heretics to indulge themselves freely without paying for the privilege with their lives, their livelihoods or their reputations. I hope this section will convey a sense of freedom and discovery. Humanists are often told by Christians and other religious people that they are wicked, selfish materialists, when in fact they are usually quiet, helpful, idealistic and considerate. It is rather satisfactory to find in these pages that important poets are on our side.

Doubt and disbelief are in everyone's experience. Four-year-olds ask what happened before God was born. Serious questions of this kind are fobbed off with embarrassed half-answers which promote uncertainty, reduce confidence and prepare the ground for passive "faith" and susceptibility to indoctrination.

Here are some of the utterances of men and women who have burst into rebellion against the censorship of parents, schools, Church and State. Here is Shelley aged 18, speaking with the indiscretion and candour of brilliant youth unaware of the reaction he will provoke. "The greater the truth, the greater the libel": the whole Establishment, legal, educational, clerical and aristocratic, will combine to ruin his life.

These poems have been arranged in chronological order, so that the ebb and flow of satire and dissent down the centuries can be traced and understood. The early critical and satirical poems operate within the framework of Christianity. They attack the excesses of the Clergy, whose power is overwhelming, so that opposition is cautious and often kept under wraps. Gradually the balance changes, until with "Dover Beach", Matthew Arnold declares the new position: the tide of faith is receding. There is a sea change. The Church is by no means dead, but it has become dimly aware of the need to moderate its treatment of dissenters.

From this point, the poems chosen are lighter in tone and content; there is a new feeling of freedom. Freud has also had his influence over the estimated value of sexual repression and the virtues of asceticism. Tennyson, had he lived fifty years later, would not have been so appalled at the idea of being descended from the Greater Apes.

But it is a mistake to think that the battle has been won. The struggle is perennial, and ground gained in one area can be lost elsewhere. The established Church may be weakened, but as Born Again Christians, astrologists, Muslims and many other groups increase in numbers and power, we surely need new satirical poets and polemical writers to maintain and enlarge the precarious Humanist influence.

Saint John Baptist

THE last and greatest Herald of Heaven's King,
   Girt with rough skins, hies to the deserts wild,
Among that savage brood the woods forth bring,
   Which he than man more harmless found and mild.
His food was locusts, and what young doth spring
   With honey that from virgin hives distilled;
Parched body, hollow eyes, some uncouth thing
   Made him appear, long since from earth exiled.
There burst he forth: "All ye, whose hopes rely
   On God, with me amidst these deserts mourn;
   Repent, repent, and from old errors turn!"
Who listened to his voice, obeyed his cry?
   Only the echoes, which he made relent,
   Rung from the marble caves "Repent! repent!"

WILLIAM DRUMMOND OF HAWTHORNDEN
(1585-1649)

The Saints

WHAT makes a knave a child of God,
And one of us?—A livelihood.
What renders beating out of brains,
And murther godliness?—Great gains.
What's tender conscience?—'Tis a botch
That will not bear the gentlest touch,
But breaking out, dispatches more
Than the epidemical'st plague-sore.
What makes y'encroach upon our trade,
And damn all others?—To be paid.
What's orthodox, and true believing
Against conscience?—A good living.
What makes rebelling against kings
A Good Old Cause?—Administ'rings.
What makes all doctrine plain and clear?
About two hundred pounds a year.
And that which was proved true before,
Prove false again?—Two hundred more.
What makes the breaking of all oaths
A holy duty?—Food, and clothes.
What laws and freedom, persecution?
Being out of power and contribution.
What makes a church a den of thieves?
A Dean, a Chapter and white sleeves.
And what would serve if those were gone,
To make it orthodox? Our own.
What makes morality a crime,
The most notorious of the time?
Morality, which both the Saints,
And wicked too, cry out against?
'Cause grace and virtue are within
Prohibited degrees of kin;
And therefore no true Saint allows,
They should be suffered to espouse;
For Saints can need no conscience
That with morality dispense;
As virtue's impious, when 'tis rooted
In Nature only, and not imputed:
But why the Wicked should do so
We neither know nor care to do.
What's liberty of conscience,

I' the natural and genuine sense?
'Tis to restore with more security,
Rebellion to its ancient purity;
And Christian liberty reduce
To th'elder practice of the Jews:
For a large conscience is all one,
And signifies the same with none.

From *Hudibras*
SAMUEL BUTLER
(1612-1680)

Priests were the first deluders of mankind

PRIESTS were the first deluders of mankind,
Who with vain faith made all their reason blind;
Not Lucifer himself more proud than they,
And yet persuade the world they must obey:
'Gainst avarice and luxury complain,
And practice all the vices they arraign.
Riches and honour they from laymen reap,
And with dull crambo feed the silly sheep.
As Killigrew buffoons his master, they
Droll on their god, but a much duller way.
With hocus-pocus, and their heavenly sleight,
They gain on tender consciences at night.
Whoever has an over-zealous wife
Becomes the priest's Amphitryo during life.
Who would such men Heaven's messengers believe,
Who from the sacred pulpit dare deceive?
Baal's wretched curates legerdemained it so,
And never durst their tricks above-board show.
When our first parents Paradise did grace,
The serpent was the prelate of the place;
Fond Eve did, for this subtle tempter's sake,
From the forbidden tree the pippin take;
His God and Lord this preacher did betray,
To have the weaker vessel made his prey.
Since death and sin did human nature blot,
The chiefest blessings Adam's chaplain got.
 Thrice wretched they, who nature's laws detest,

To taste the ways fantastic of a priest,
Till native reason's basely forced to yield,
And hosts of upstart errors gain the field..

From *An Historical Poem*
ANDREW MARVELL
(1621-1678)

Confessio Fidei

WHAT weight of ancient witness can prevail,
If private reason hold the public scale?
But, gracious God, how well dost thou provide
For erring judgments an unerring guide!
Thy throne is darkness in the abyss of light,
A blaze of glory that forbids the sight.
O teach me to believe thee thus concealed,
And search no further than thyself revealed;
But her alone for my director take
Whom thou hast promised never to forsake!
My thoughtless youth was winged with vain desires;
My manhood, long misled by wandering fires,
Followed false lights; and when their glimpse was gone
My pride struck out new sparkles of her own.
Such was I, such by nature still I am;
Be thine the glory and be mine the shame!
Good life be now my task; my doubts are done;
What more could fright my faith than Three in One?
Can I believe eternal God could lie
Disguised in mortal mould and infancy,
That the great Maker of the world could die?
And, after that, trust my imperfect sense
Which calls in question his omnipotence?
Can I my reason to my faith compel,
And shall my sight and touch and taste rebel?
Superior faculties are set aside;
Shall their subservient organs be my guide?
Then let the moon usurp the rule of day,
And winking tapers show the sun his way;
For what my senses can themselves perceive
I need no revelation to believe.

JOHN DRYDEN
(1631-1700)

A Satire Against Reason and Mankind

WERE I (who to my cost already am
One of those strange, prodigious creatures, man)
A spirit free to choose, for my own share,
What case of flesh and blood I pleased to wear,
I'd be a dog, a monkey, or a bear,
Or anything but that vain animal
Who is so proud of being rational.
   The senses are too gross, and he'll contrive
A sixth, to contradict the other five,
And before certain instinct, will prefer
Reason, which fifty times for one does err:
Reason, an *ignis fatuus* in the mind
Which, leaving light of nature, sense, behind,
Pathless and dangerous wandering ways it takes
Through error's fenny bogs and thorny brakes;
Whilst the misguided follower climbs with pain
Mountains of whimseys, heaped in his own brain;
Stumbling from thought to thought, falls headlong down
Into doubt's boundless sea, where, like to drown,
Books bear him up awhile, and make him try
To swim with bladders of philosophy;
In hopes still to o'ertake th'escaping light,
The vapour dances in his dazzling sight
Till, spent, it leaves him to eternal night.
Then old age and experience, hand in hand,
Lead him to death, and make him understand,
After a search so painful and so long,
That all his life he has been in the wrong.
Huddled in dirt the reasoning engine lies
Who was so proud, so witty, and so wise.
   Pride drew him in, as cheats their bubbles catch,
And made him venture to be made a wretch.
His wisdom did his happiness destroy,
Aiming to know that world he should enjoy.
And wit was his vain, frivolous pretence,
Of pleasing others at his own expense,
For wits are treated just like common whores:
First they're enjoyed, and then kicked out of doors.
The pleasure past, a threatening doubt remains
That frights th'enjoyer with succeeding pains
   Women and men of wit are dangerous tools,

And ever fatal to admiring fools;
Pleasure allures, and when the fops escape,
'Tis not that they're belov'd, but fortunate,
And therefore what they fear at heart, they hate.
    But now, methinks, some formal band and beard
Takes me to task. Come on, sir; I'm prepared.
    "Then, by your favour, anything that's writ
Against this gibing, jingling knack called wit
Likes me abundantly; but you take care
Upon this point, not to be too severe.
Perhaps my muse were fitter for this part,
For I profess I can be very smart
On wit, which I abhor with all my heart.
I long to lash it in some sharp essay,
But your grand indiscretion bids me stay
And turns my tide of ink another way.
    "What rage ferments in your degenerate mind
To make you rail at reason and mankind?
Blest, glorious man! to whom alone kind heaven
An everlasting soul has freely given,
Whom his great Maker took such care to make
That from himself he did the image take
And this fair frame in shining reason dressed
To dignify his nature above beast;
Reason, by whose aspiring influence
We take a flight beyond material sense,
Dive into mysteries, then soaring pierce
The flaming limits of the universe,
Search heaven and hell, find out what's acted there,
And give the world true grounds of hope and fear."
    Hold, mighty man, I cry, all this we know
From the pathetic pen of Ingelo,
From Patrick's *Pilgrim*, Sibbes' soliloquies,
And 'tis this very reason I despise:
This supernatural gift, that makes a mite
Think he's the image of the infinite,
Comparing his short life, void of all rest,
To the eternal and the ever blest;
This busy, puzzling stirrer-up of doubt
That frames deep mysteries, then finds 'em out,
Filling with frantic crowds of thinking fools
Those reverend bedlams, colleges and schools;
Borne on whose wings, each heavy sot can pierce

The limits of the boundless universe;
So charming ointments make an old witch fly
And bear a crippled carcass through the sky.
'Tis this exalted power, whose business lies
In nonsense and impossibilities,
This made a whimsical philosopher
Before the spacious world, his tub prefer,
And we have modern cloistered coxcombs who
Retire to think, 'cause they have nought to do.
But thoughts are given for action's government;
Where action ceases, thought's impertinent.
Our sphere of action is life's happiness,
And he who thinks beyond, thinks like an ass.
Thus, whilst against false reasoning I inveigh,
I own right reason, which I would obey:
That reason which distinguishes by sense
And gives us rules of good and ill from thence,
That bounds desires with a reforming will
To keep 'em more in vigour, not to kill.
Your reason hinders, mine helps to enjoy,
Renewing appetites yours would destroy.
My reason is my friend, yours is a cheat;
Hunger calls out, my reason bids me eat;
Perversely, yours your appetite does mock:
This asks for food, that answers, "What's o'clock?"
This plain distinction, sir, your doubt secures:
'Tis not true reason I despise, but yours.
Thus I think reason righted, but for man,
I'll ne'er recant; defend him if you can.
For all his pride and his philosophy,
'Tis evident beasts are, in their degree,
As wise at least, and better far than he.
Those creatures are the wisest who attain,
By surest means, the ends at which they aim.
If therefore Jowler finds and kills his hares
Better than Meres supplies committee chairs,
Though one's a statesman, th'other but a hound,
Jowler, in justice, would be wiser found.
You see how far man's wisdom here extends;
Look next if human nature makes amends:
Whose principles most generous are, and just,
And to whose morals you would sooner trust.
Be judge yourself, I'll bring it to the test:

Which is the basest creature, man or beast?
Birds feed on birds, beasts on each other prey,
But savage man alone does man betray.
Pressed by necessity, they kill for food;
Man undoes man to do himself no good.
With teeth and claws by nature armed, they hunt
Nature's allowance, to supply their want.
But man, with smiles, embraces, friendship, praise,
Inhumanly his fellow's life betrays;
With voluntary pains works his distress,
Not through necessity, but wantonness.
   For hunger or for love they fight and tear,
Whilst wretched man is still in arms for fear.
For fear he arms, and is of arms afraid,
By fear to fear successively betrayed;
Base fear, the source whence his best passions came:
His boasted honour, and his dear-bought fame;
That lust of power, to which he's such a slave,
And for which alone he dares be brave;
To which his various projects are designed;
Which makes him generous, affable, and kind;
For which he takes such pains to be thought wise,
And screws his actions in a forced disguise,
Leading a tedious life in misery
Under laborious, mean hypocrisy.
   Look to the bottom of his vast design,
Wherein man's wisdom, power, and glory join:
The good he acts, the ill he does endure,
'Tis all from fear, to make himself secure.
Merely for safety, after fame we thirst,
For all men would be cowards if they durst.
   And honesty's against all common sense:
Men must be knaves, 'tis in their own defence.
Mankind's dishonest; if you think it fair
Amongst known cheats to play upon the square,
You'll be undone.
Nor can weak truth your reputation save:
The knaves will all agree to call you knave.
Wronged shall he live, insulted o'er, oppressed,
Who dares be less a villain than the rest.
   Thus, sir, you see what human nature craves:
Most men are cowards, all men should be knaves.
The difference lies, as far as I can see,

Not in the thing itself, but the degree,
And all the subject matter of debate
Is only: Who's a knave of the first rate?

All this with indignation have I hurled
At the pretending part of the proud world,
Who, swollen with selfish vanity, devise
False freedoms, holy cheats, and formal lies
Over their fellow slaves to tyrannize.
But if in Court so just a man there be
(In Court a just man, yet unknown to me)
Who does his needful flattery direct,
Not to oppress and ruin, but protect
(Since flattery, which way soever laid,
Is still a tax on that unhappy trade);
If so upright a statesman you can find,
Whose passions bend to his unbiased mind,
Who does his arts and policies apply
To raise his country, not his family,
Nor, whilst his pride owned avarice withstands,
Receives close bribes through friends' corrupted hands—
Is there a churchman who on God relies;
Whose life, his faith and doctrine justifies?
Not one blown up with vain prelatic pride,
Who, for reproof of sins, does man deride;
Whose envious heart makes preaching a pretence,
With his obstreperous, saucy eloquence,
To chide at kings, and rail at men of sense;
None of that sensual tribe whose talents lie
In avarice, pride, sloth, and gluttony;
Who hunt good livings, but abhor good lives;
Whose lust exalted to that height arrives
They act adultery with their own wives,
And ere a score of years completed be,
Can from the lofty pulpit proudly see
Half a large parish their own progeny;
Nor doting bishop who would be adored
For domineering at the council board,
A greater fop in business at fourscore,
Fonder of serious toys, affected more,
Than the gay, glittering fool at twenty proves
With all his noise, his tawdry clothes, and loves;
But a meek, humble man of honest sense,

Who, preaching peace, does practice continence;
Whose pious life's a proof he does believe
Mysterious truths, which no man can conceive.
If upon earth there dwell such God-like men,
I'll here recant my paradox to them,
Adore those shrines of virtue, homage pay,
And, with the rabble' world, their laws obey.
    If such there be, yet grant me this at least:
Man differs more from man, than man from beast.

JOHN WILMOT, EARL OF ROCHESTER
(1647-1680)

Science! thou fair effusive ray . . .

SCIENCE! thou fair effusive ray
From the great source of mental day,
Free, generous, and refined!
Illumine each bewildered thought,
And bless my labouring mind.

But first with thy resistless light,
Disperse those phantoms from my sight,
Those mimic shades of thee;
The scholiast's learning, sophist's cant,
The visionary bigot's rant,
The monk's philosophy.

From *Hymn to Science*
MARK AKENSIDE
(1721-1770)

Mounting the Church-Ladder

THE FATHER, who designs his babe as priest,
Dreams him episcopally such at least;
And, while the playful jockey scours the room
Briskly, astride upon the parlour broom,
In fancy sees him more superbly ride

In coach with purple lined, and mitres on its side.
Events improbable and strange as these,
Which only a parental eye foresees,
A public school shall bring to pass with ease.
But how! resides such virtue in that air
As must create an appetite for prayer?
And will it breathe into him all the zeal
That candidates for such a prize should feel,
To take the lead and be the foremost still
In all true worth and literary skill?
Ah, blind to bright futurity, untaught
The knowledge of the world, and dull of thought!
Church-ladders are not always mounted best
By learned clerks and Latinists professed.
Th'exalted prize demands an upward look,
Not to be found by poring on a book.
Small skill in Latin, and still less in Greek,
Is more than adequate to all I seek.
Let erudition grace him or not grace,
I give the bauble but the second place;
His wealth, fame, honours, all that I intend,
Subsist and centre in one point—a friend!
A friend, what e'er he studies or neglects,
Shall give him consequence, heal all defects.
His intercourse with peers, and sons of peers —
There dawns the splendour of his future years;
In that bright quarter his propitious skies
Shall blush betimes, and there his glory rise.
Your Lordship, and Your Grace! what school can teach
A rhet'ric equal to those parts of speech?
What need of Homer's verse or Tully's prose,
Sweet interjections! if he learn but those?
Let rev'rend churls his ignorance rebuke,
Who starve upon a dog's eared Pentateuch,
The parson knows enough who knows a duke.

From *Tirciconium: or a Review of Schools*
WILLIAM COWPER
(1731-1800)

Inebriety

THE vicar at the table's front presides,
Whose presence a monastic life derides;
The reverend wig, in sideway order placed,
The reverend band, by rubric stains disgraced,
The leering eye, 'in wayward circles roll'd,
Mark him the pastor of a jovial fold,
Whose various texts excite a loud applause,
Favouring the bottle, and the good old cause.
See! the dull smile which fearfully appears,
When gross indecency her front uprears,
The joy conceal'd, the fiercer burns within,
As masks afford the keenest gust to sin;
Imagination helps the reverend sire,
And spreads the sails of sub-divine desire;
But when the gay immoral joke goes round,
When shame and all her blushing train are drown'd,
Rather than hear his God blasphemed, he takes
The last loved glass, and then the board forsakes.
Not that religion prompts the sober thought,
But slavish custom has the practice taught;
Besides, this zealous son of warm devotion
Has a true Levite bias for promotion.
Vicars must with discretion go astray,
Whilst bishops may be damn'd the nearest way;
So puny robbers individuals kill,
When hector-heroes murder as they will.

From *Inebriety: a poem*
GEORGE CRABBE
(1754-1832)

The Garden of Love

I WENT to the Garden of Love,
And saw what I never had seen:
A Chapel was built in the midst,
Where I used to play on the green.

And the gates of this Chapel were shut,
And "Thou shalt not" writ over the door;
So I turn'd to the Garden of Love
That so many sweet flowers bore;

And I saw it was filled with graves,
And tomb-stones where flowers should be;
And priests in black gowns were walking their
    rounds,
And binding with briars my joys and desires.

WILLIAM BLAKE
(1757-1827)

From Don Juan

CANTO XI

I

WHEN Bishop Berkeley said "there was no matter,"
    And proved it—'twas no matter what he said:
They say his system 'tis in vain to batter,
    Too subtle for the airiest human head;
And yet who can believe it? I would shatter
    Gladly all matters down to stone or lead,
Or adamant, to find the world a spirit,
And wear my head, denying that I wear it.

II

What a sublime discovery 'twas to make the
   Universe universal egotism,
That's all ideal—all *ourselves*! I'll stake the
   World (be it what you will) that *that's* no schism:
Oh Doubt!—if thou be'st Doubt, for which some
                                 take thee,
   But which I doubt extremely—thou sole prism
Of the Truth's rays, spoil not my draught of spirit!
Heaven's brandy, though our brain can hardly bear it.

III

For ever and anon comes Indigestion
   (Not the most "dainty Ariel"), and perplexes
Our soarings with another sort of question:
   And that which after all my spirit vexes,
Is, that I find no spot where man can rest eye on,
   Without confusion of the sorts and sexes,
Of beings, stars, and this unriddled wonder,
The world, which at the worst's a *glorious* blunder,

IV

If it be chance; or if it be according
   To the old text, still better:—lest it should
Turn out so, we'll say nothing 'gainst the wording,
   As several people think such hazards rude.
They're right; our days are too brief for affording
   Space to dispute what *no one* ever could
Decide, and *everybody one day will*
Know very clearly—or at least lie still.

V

And therefore will I leave off metaphysical
   Discussion, which is neither here nor there:
If I agree that what is, is; this then I call
   Being quite perspicuous and extremely fair;
The truth is, I've grown lately rather phthisical;
   I don't know what the reason is—the air
Perhaps; but as I suffer from the shocks
Of illness, I grow much more orthodox.

VI

The first attack at once proved the Divinity
(But *that* I never doubted, nor the Devil):
The next, the Virgin's mystical virginity;
The third, the usual Origin of Evil;
The fourth at once establish'd the whole Trinity
On so uncontrovertible a level,
That I devoutly wish'd the three were four
On purpose to believe so much the more.

LORD BYRON
(1788-1824)

Queen Mab

VII

SPIRIT

I WAS an infant when my mother went
To see an atheist burned. She took me there:
The dark-robed priests were met around the pile;
The multitude was gazing silently;
And as the culprit passed with dauntless mien,
Tempered disdain in his unaltering eye,
Mixed with a quiet smile, shone calmly forth:
The thirsty fire crept round his manly limbs;
His resolute eyes were scorched to blindness soon;
His death-pang rent my heart! the insensate mob
Uttered a cry of triumph, and I wept.
Weep not, child! cried my mother, for that man
Has said, There is no God.

FAIRY

There is no God!
Nature confirms the faith his death-groan sealed:
Let heaven and earth, let man's revolving race,
His ceaseless generations tell their tale;
Let every part depending on the chain
That links it to the whole, point to the hand

That grasps its term! let every seed that falls
In silent eloquence unfold its store
Of argument: infinity within,
Infinity without, belie creation;
The exterminable spirit it contains
Is nature's only God; but human pride
Is skilful to invent most serious names
To hide its ignorance.
　　　　The name of God
Has fenced about all crime with holiness,
Himself the creature of his worshippers,
Whose names and attributes and passions change,
Seeva, Buddh, Foh, Jehovah, God, or Lord,
Even with the human dupes who built his shrines,
Still serving o'er the war-polluted world
For desolation's watchword; whether hosts
Stain his death-blushing chariot-wheels, as on
Triumphantly they roll, whilst Brahmins raise
A sacred hymn to mingle with the groans;
Or countless partners of his power divide
His tyranny to weakness; or the smoke
Of burning towns, the cries of female helplessness,
Unarmed old age, and youth, and infancy,
Horribly massacred, ascend to heaven
In honour of his name; or, last and worst,
Earth groans beneath religion's iron age,
And priests dare babble of a God of peace,
Even whilst their hands are red with guiltless blood,
Murdering the while, uprooting every germ
Of truth, exterminating, spoiling all,
Making the earth a slaughter-house!

From *Queen Mab*
PERCY BYSSHE SHELLEY
(1792-1822)

Written in Disgust of Vulgar Superstition

THE church bells toll a melancholy round,
  Calling the people to some other prayers,
  Some other gloominess, more dreadful cares,
More hearkening to the sermon's horrid sound.
Surely the mind of man is closely bound
  In some black spell; seeing that each one tears
  Himself from fireside joys, and Lydian airs,
And converse high of those with glory crown'd.
Still, still they toll, and I should feel a damp,—
  A chill as from a tomb, did I not know
That they are dying like an outburnt lamp;
  That 'tis their sighing, wailing ere they go
  Into oblivion;—that fresh flowers will grow,
And many glories of immortal stamp.

JOHN KEATS
(1795-1821)

From In Memoriam

LIII

HOLD thou the good: define it well:
  For fear divine Philosophy
  Should push beyond her mark, and be
Procuress to the Lords of Hell.

LIV

Oh yet we trust that somehow good
  Will be the final goal of ill,
  To pangs of nature, sins of will,
Defects of doubt, and taints of blood.

That not a worm is cloven in vain;
  That not a moth with vain desire
  Is shrivell'd in a fruitless fire,
Or but subserves another's gain.

Behold, we know not anything;
   I can but trust that good shall fall
   At last—far off—at last, to all,
And every winter change to spring.

So runs my dream: but what am I?
   An infant crying in the night:
   An infant crying for the light:
And with no language but a cry.

LV

The wish, that of the living whole
   No life may fail beyond the grave,
   Derives it not from what we have
The likest God within the soul?

Are God and Nature then at strife,
   That Nature lends such evil dreams?
   So careful of the type she seems,
So careless of the single life;

That I, considering everywhere
   Her secret meaning in her deeds,
   And finding that of fifty seeds
She often brings but one to bear,

I falter where I firmly trod,
   And falling with my weight of cares
   Upon the great world's altar-stairs
That slope through darkness up to God,

I stretch lame hands of faith, and grope,
   And gather dust and chaff, and call
   To what I feel is Lord of all,
And faintly trust the larger hope.

LVI

"So careful of the type?" but no.
   From scarped cliff and quarried stone
   She cries, "A thousand types are gone:
I care for nothing, all shall go.

"Thou makest thine appeal to me:
    I bring to life, I bring to death:
    The spirit does but mean the breath:
I know no more." And he, shall he,

Man, her last work, who seemed so fair,
    Such splendid purpose in his eyes,
    Who roll'd the psalm to wintry skies,
Who built him fanes of fruitless prayer,

Who trusted God was love indeed
    And love Creation's final law —
    Tho' Nature, red in tooth and claw
With ravine, shriek'd against his creed —

Who loved, who suffer'd countless ills,
    Who battled for the True, the Just,
    Be blown about the desert dust,
Or seal'd within the iron hills?

No more? A monster then, a dream,
    A discord. Dragons of the prime,
    That tear each other in their slime,
Were mellow music match'd with him.

O life as futile, then, as frail!
    O far thy voice to soothe and bless!
    What hope of answer or redress?
Behind the veil, behind the veil.

CXX

I trust I have not wasted breath:
    I think we are not wholly brain,
    Magnetic mockeries; not in vain,
Like Paul with beasts, I fought with Death;

Not only cunning casts in clay:
    Let Science prove we are, and then
    What matters Science unto men,
At least to me? I would not stay.

Let him, the wiser man who springs
   Hereafter, up from childhood shape
   His action like the greater ape,
But I was *born* to other things.

From *In Memoriam*
ALFRED TENNYSON
(1809-1892)

The Latest Decalogue

THOU shalt have one God only; who
Would be at the expense of two?
No graven images may be
Worshipped, except the currency:
Swear not at all; for, for thy curse
Thine enemy is none the worse:
At church on Sunday to attend
Will serve to keep the world thy friend:
Honour thy parents; that is, all
From whom advancement may befall:
Thou shalt not kill; but needst not strive
Officiously to keep alive:
Do not adultery commit;
Advantage rarely comes of it.
Thou shalt not steal; an empty feat,
When it's so lucrative to cheat:
Bear not false witness; let the lie
Have time on its own wings to fly:
Thou shalt not covet; but tradition
Approves all forms of competition.

ARTHUR H. CLOUGH
(1819-1861)

Dover Beach

THE sea is calm to-night.
The tide is full, the moon lies fair
Upon the straits;—on the French coast the light
Gleams and is gone; the cliffs of England stand,
Glimmering and vast, out in the tranquil bay.
Come to the window, sweet is the night-air!

Only, from the long line of spray
Where the sea meets the moon-blanch'd land,
Listen! you hear the grating roar
Of pebbles which the waves draw back, and fling,
At their return, up the high strand,
Begin, and cease, and then again begin,
With tremulous cadence slow, and bring
The eternal note of sadness in.

Sophocles long ago
Heard it on the Aegean, and it brought
Into his mind the turbid ebb and flow
Of human misery; we
Find also in the sound a thought,
Hearing it by this distant northern sea.

The Sea of Faith
Was once, too, at the full, and round earth's shore
Lay like the folds of a bright girdle furl'd.
But now I only hear
Its melancholy, long, withdrawing roar,
Retreating, to the breath
Of the night-wind, down the vast edges drear
And naked shingles of the world.

Ah, love, let us be true
To one another! for the world, which seems
To lie before us like a land of dreams,
So various, so beautiful, so new,
Hath really neither joy, nor love, nor light,
Nor certitude, nor peace, nor help for pain;
And we are here as on a darkling plain
Swept with confused alarms of struggle and flight,
While ignorant armies clash by night.

MATTHEW ARNOLD
(1822-1888)

Mimnermus in Church

YOU promise heavens free from strife,
   Pure truth, and perfect change of will;
But sweet, sweet is this human life,
   So sweet, I fain would breathe it still;
Your chilly stars I can forgo,
This warm kind world is all I know.

You say there is no substance here,
   One great reality above:
Back from that void I shrink in fear,
   And child-like hide myself in love:
Show me what angels feel. Till then
I cling, a mere weak man, to men.

You bid me lift my mean desires
   From faltering lips and fitful veins
To sexless souls, ideal quires,
   Unwearied voices, wordless strains:
My mind with fonder welcome owns
One dear dead friend's remember'd tones.

Forsooth the present we must give
   To that which cannot pass away;
All beauteous things for which we live
   By laws of time and space decay.
But Oh, the very reason why
I clasp them, is because they die.

WILLIAM JOHNSON CORY
(1823-1892)

Parting

MY life closed twice before its close;
   It yet remains to see
If Immortality unveil
   A third event to me

So huge, so hopeless to conceive,
   As these that twice befell.
Parting is all we know of heaven,
   And all we need of hell.

EMILY DICKINSON
(1830-1886)

A Plaint to Man

WHEN you slowly emerged from the den of Time,
And gained percipience as you grew,
And fleshed you fair out of shapeless slime,

Wherefore, O Man, did there come to you
The unhappy need of creating me —
A form like your own—for praying to?

My virtue, power, utility,
Within my maker must all abide,
Since none in myself can ever be,

One thin as a phasm on a lantern-slide
Shown forth in the dark upon some dim sheet,
And by none but its showman vivified.

"Such a forced device", you may say, "is meet
For easing a loaded heart at whiles:
Man needs to conceive of a mercy-seat

"Somewhere above the gloomy aisles
Of this wailful world, or he could not bear
The irk no local hope beguiles."

— But since I was framed in your first despair
The doing without me has had no play
In the minds of men when shadows scare;

And now that I dwindle day by day
Beneath the deicide eyes of seers
In a light that will not let me stay,

And tomorrow the whole of me disappears,
The truth should be told, and the fact be faced
That had best been faced in earlier years:

The fact of life with dependence placed
On the human heart's resource alone,
In brotherhood bonded close and graced

With loving-kindness fully blown,
And visioned help unsought, unknown.

THOMAS HARDY
(1840-1928)

Vagabond

DUNNO a heap about what an' why,
    Can't say's I ever knowed.
Heaven to me's a fair blue stretch of sky,
    Earth's jest a dusty road.

Dunno the names o' things, nor what they are,
    Can't say's I ever will.
Dunno about God—He's jest the noddin' star
    Atop the windy hill.

Dunno about Life—it's jest a tramp alone
    From wakin'-time to doss.
Dunno about Death—it's jest a quiet stone
    All over-grey wi' moss.

An' why I live, an' why the old world spins,
    Are things I never knowed;
My mark's the gypsy fires, the lonely inns,
    An' jest the dusty road.

JOHN MASEFIELD
(1878-1967)

February Afternoon

MEN heard this roar of parleying starlings, saw,
   A thousand years ago even as now,
   Black rooks with white gulls following the plough
So that the first are last until a caw
Commands that last are first again,—a law
   Which was of old when one, like me, dreamed how
   A thousand years might dust lie on his brow
Yet thus would birds do between hedge and shaw.

Time swims before me, making as a day
   A thousand years, while the broad ploughland oak
   Roars mill-like and men strike and bear the stroke
   Of war as ever, audacious or resigned,
And God still sits aloft in the array
   That we have wrought him, stone-deaf and
                                    stone-blind.

EDWARD THOMAS
(1878-1917)

"They"

THE Bishop tells us: "When the boys come back
They will not be the same; for they'll have fought
In a just cause: they lead the last attack
On Anti-Christ; their comrades' blood has bought
New right to breed an honourable race,
They have challenged Death and dared him face to
                                    face."

"We're none of us the same!" the boys reply.
"For George lost both his legs; and Bill's stone blind;
Poor Jim's shot through the lungs and like to die;
And Bert's gone syphilitic: you'll not find
A chap who's served that hasn't found *some* change."
And the Bishop said: "The ways of God are strange!"

SIEGFRIED SASSOON
(1886-1967)

Heaven

FISH (fly-replete, in depth of June,
Dawdling away their wat'ry noon)
Ponder deep wisdom, dark or clear,
Each secret fishy hope or fear.
Fish say, they have their Stream and Pond;
But is there anything Beyond?
This life cannot be All, they swear,
For how unpleasant, if it were!
One may not doubt that, somehow, Good
Shall come of Water and of Mud;
And, sure, the reverent eye must see
A Purpose in Liquidity.
We darkly know, by Faith we cry,
The future is not Wholly Dry.
Mud unto mud!—Death eddies near—
Not here the appointed End, not here!
But somewhere, beyond Space and Time,
Is wetter water, slimier slime!
And there (they trust) there swimmeth One
Who swam ere rivers were begun,
Immense, of fishy form and mind,
Squamous, omnipotent, and kind;
And under that Almighty Fin,
The littlest fish may enter in.
Oh! never fly conceals a hook,
Fish say, in the Eternal Brook,
But more than mundane weeds are there,
And mud, celestially fair;
Fat caterpillars drift around,
And paradisal grubs are found;
Unfading moths, immortal flies,
And the worm that never dies.
And in that Heaven of all their wish,
There shall be no more land, say fish.

RUPERT BROOKE
(1887-1915)

At the Graveside

THERE is no stupid soul who neither knows
The rudiments of human history
Nor seeks to solve the problems of this life
But still must give his witless testimony
On huge conundrums.—Faithless in small things,
Let all such cease their fond imaginings.
The eyes of fools are on the ends of God.
I postpone all such thoughts beneath this sod.

HUGH MACDIARMID
(1892-1978)

The End

AFTER the blast of lightning in the east,
The flourish of loud clouds, the Chariot Throne;
After the drums of time have rolled and ceased,
And by the bronze west long retreat is blown,

Shall Life renew these bodies? Of a truth
All death will he annul, all tears assuage?—
Or fill these void veins full again with youth,
And wash with an immortal water, Age?

When I do ask white Age he saith not so:
"My head hangs weighed with snow."
And when I hearken to the Earth, she saith:
"My fiery heart shrinks, aching. It is death.
Mine ancient scars shall not be glorified,
Nor my titanic tears, the seas, be dried."

WILFRED OWEN
(1893-1918)

Sonnet

WHEN you see millions of the mouthless dead
Across your dreams in pale battalions go,
Say not soft things as other men have said,
That you'll remember. For you need not so.
Give them not praise. For, deaf, how should they know
It is not curses heaped on each gashed head?
Nor tears. Their blind eyes see not your tears flow.
Nor honour. It is easy to be dead.
Say only this, "They are dead." Then add thereto,
"Yet many a better one has died before."
Then, scanning all the o'ercrowded mass, should you
Perceive one face that you loved heretofore,
It is a spook. None wears the face you knew.
Great death has made all his for evermore.

CHARLES SORLEY
(1895-1915)

Do I Believe?

Do I believe in God?
Well yes, I suppose, in a sort of way;
It's really terribly hard to say.
I'm sure that there must be, of course,
Some kind of vital, motive force,
Some power that holds the winning cards
Behind life's ambiguous facades,
But whether you think me odd or not
I can't decide if it's God or not.

I look at the changing sea and sky
And try to picture eternity.
I gaze at immensities of blue
And say to myself ''It can't be true
That somewhere up in that abstract sphere
Are all the people who once were here,
Attired in white and shapeless gowns
Sitting on clouds like eiderdowns
Plucking at harps and twanging lutes
With cherubim in their birthday suits,
Set in an ageless, timeless dream
Part of a formulated scheme
Formulated before the Flood
Before the amoeba left the mud
And, stranded upon a rocky shelf
Proceeded to subdivide itself.''

I look at the changing sea and sky
And try to picture infinity;
I gaze at a multitude of stars
Envisaging the men on Mars,
Wondering if they too are torn
Between their sunset and their dawn
By dreadful night-engendered fears
Of what may lie beyond their years
And if they too, through thick and thin,
Are dogged by consciousness of Sin.

Have they, to give them self-reliance,
A form of Martian Christian Science?
Or do they live in constant hope
Of dispensations from some Pope?
Are they pursued from womb to tomb
By hideous prophecies of doom?
Have they cathedral, church or chapel?
Are they concerned with Adam's Apple?
Have they immortal souls like us
Or are they—less presumptuous?

NOEL COWARD
(1899-1973)

The Past

PEOPLE who are always praising the past
And especially the times of faith as best
Ought to go and live in the Middle Ages
And be burnt at the stake as witches and sages.

STEVIE SMITH
(1902-1971)

Was He Married?

WAS he married, did he try
To support as he grew less fond of them
Wife and family?

No,
He never suffered such a blow.

Did he feel pointless, feeble and distrait,
Unwanted by everyone and in the way?

From his cradle he was purposeful,
His bent strong and his mind full.

Did he love people very much
Yet find them die one day?

He did not love them in the human way.

Did he ask how long it would go on,
Wonder if Death could be counted on for an end?

He did not feel like this,
He had a future of bliss.

Did he never feel strong
Pain for being wrong?

He was not wrong, he was right,
He suffered from others', not his own, spite.

But there *is* no suffering like having made a mistake
Because of being of an inferior make.

He was not inferior,
He was superior.

He knew then that power corrupts but some must
    govern?
His thoughts were different.

Did he lack friends? Worse,
Think it was for his fault, not theirs?

He did not lack friends,
He had disciples he moulded to his ends.

Did he feel over-handicapped sometimes, yet must
    draw even?

How could he feel like this? He was the King of
    Heaven.

Did he find a sudden brightness one day in
    everything?
Because a mood had been conquered, or a sin?

I tell you he did not sin.

Do only human beings suffer from the irritation
I have mentioned? learn too that being comical
Does not ameliorate the desperation?

Only human beings feel this,
It is because they are so mixed.

All human beings should have a medal,
A god cannot carry it, he is not able.

A god is Man's doll, you ass,
He makes him up like this on purpose.

He might have made him up worse.

He often has, in the past.

To choose a god of love, as he did and does,
Is a little move then?

Yes, it is.

A larger one will be when men
Love love and hate hate but do not deify them?

It will be a larger one.

STEVIE SMITH

What are They Thinking . . .

WHAT are they thinking, the people in churches,
Closing their eyelids and kneeling to pray,
Touching their faces and sniffing their fingers,
Folding their knuckles one over another?
What are they thinking? Do they remember
This is the church: and this is the steeple:
Open the door: and here are the people?
Do they still see the parson climbing upstairs,
Opening the window and saying his prayers?

Do they perceive in the pit of their palms
The way of the walls and the spin of the spire,
The turmoil of tombstones tossed in the grass,
Under the yawning billows of yew?
Can they discover, drooping beyond them,
The chestnuts' fountains of flowers and frills,
And the huge fields folded into the hills?

What are they thinking, the sheep on the hills,
Bobbing and bending to nibble the grass,
Kissing the crisp green coat of the combes?
What are they thinking, lying contented
With vacant regard in long rumination?
Do they consider the sky as a cage,
Their fleeces as fetters, their bones as their bonds?
Or do they rejoice at the thyme on their tongues,
The dome of the sky, the slope of the downs,
The village below, the church, and the steeple,
With shepherd and ploughman and parson and people?

And what is he feeling, the lark as he flies,
Does he consider the span of his days,
Does he dissever himself from his spirit, .
His flight from his feathers, his song from his singing?
Is he cast down at the thought of his brevity?
Or does he look forward to fond immortality?
He stitches the sky with the thread of his breath
To all the bright pattern of living beneath
To ploughman and shepherd and parson and people,
To the sheep on the hills and the church and the
  steeple.

BRYAN GUINNESS
(1905-   )

The Day After Sunday

ALWAYS on Monday, God's in the morning papers,
  His Name is a headline, His Works are rumoured
  abroad.
Having been praised by men who are movers and
  shapers,
  From prominent Sunday pulpits, newsworthy is God.

On page 27, just opposite Fashion Trends,
  One reads at a glance how He scolded the Baptists a
  little,
Was firm with the Catholics, practical with the Friends,
  To Unitarians pleasantly noncommittal.

In print are His numerous aspects, too: God smiling,
  God vexed, God thunderous, God Whose mansions
  are pearl,
Political God, God frugal, God reconciling
  Himself with science, God guiding the Camp Fire
  Girl.

Always on Monday morning the press reports
  God as revealed to His vicars in various guises —
Benevolent, stormy, patient, or out of sorts.
  God knows which God is the God God recognises.

PHYLLIS MCGINLEY
(1905-   )

How to Start a War

SAID Zwingli to Muntzer,
"I'll have to be blunt, sir.
I don't like your version
Of Total Immersion.
And since God's on my side
And I'm on the dry side,
You'd better swing ovah
To me and Jehovah."

Cried Muntzer, "It's schism,
Is Infant Baptism!
Since I've had a sign, sir,
That God's will is mine, sir,
Let all men agree
With Jehovah and me,
Or go to Hell, singly,"
Said Muntzer to Zwingli,

As each drew his sword
On the side of the Lord.

PHYLLIS MCGINLEY

State Meeting at Jerusalem

AND went you to Jerusalem
To greet your risen Lord?
And found you rooms at Bethlehem
At rates you could afford?
And walked you to Gethsemane
Along the road He trod,
To hail the risen glory
Of the Son of man and God?

84

Oh I went to Jerusalem,
But all the Lords I met
Were King and Pope and Patriarch,
Who came by car and jet;
And stable room at Bethlehem
Was fetching wealth untold,
And parking space at Nazareth
Could not be bought for gold.

But found you in Jerusalem
An answer to your need? —
I found an empty sepulchre,
I found an empty creed.
I found no Christ among the crowds
That thronged the streets that hour:
I found the Kingdom bartered
For the Glory and the Power.

PHYLLIS FFORDE
(1907-1987)

Exclusion and Acceptance

WHO rejects all new ideas
    Turns the infant from the door,
Curbing with his inner fears
    Those who venture to explore.

To his house he enters in,
    Lets his Self expand and grow,
Calls it God, the Other, Sin:
    God is all, all else is woe.

God is then exalted high,
    Light and angels round him shine
And in his great vaulted sky
    Gleams the perfect soul divine.

But below the eye discerns
   Horizontally outspread
Clouds, and far beneath them turns
   Earth in grief, bestrewn with dead.

Under Earth's concealing crust
   Hornèd devils feed the fires;
Ash to ashes, dust to dust
   Flesh must go, and all desires.

Flesh is sin, Desires are flame,
   But, whatever Self decrees,
Flesh survives and makes its claim
   And Desires conspire to tease.

★   ★   ★

Who accepts the new ideas
   Bids the infant enter in;
God descends, and selfly fears
   Fade when flesh no more is sin.

God and Devil then unite,
   From their union Man appears;
Sun and Day, and Moon and Night
   Greet him, and allay his fears.

Gone are Hell and Devils grim;
   Woman now gives happy birth;
Child and woman step with him
   Through the sad and merry earth.

BET CHERRINGTON
(1912-   )

Facing East

BOGUS! Bogus! Bogus! Lord God Almighty
No indeed we don't believe the half of what we say;
Bogus! Bogus! Bogus! Merciful and mighty,
All we want is much more cash and let the weaker pay!

Bogus! Bogus! Bogus! All the saints adore Thee;
Such poor mugs as they once were O grant us not to be!
Cherubim and Seraphim falling down before Thee
Hadn't learnt that double-think can set the conscience
   free!

Bogus! Bogus! Bogus! Tho' the darkness hide Thee,
Tho' we doubt if Thou art there there's no security!
Possibly Thou know'st us and our bad intentions,
So we put our money in to buy immunity.

Bogus! Bogus! Bogus! Lord God Almighty,
Let us take in vain Thy name with true hypocrisy;
Mental reservations enable us to call Thee
God in Three Persons, blessèd Trinity!

BET CHERRINGTON

Song of the Bishop of Woolwich:
"Our Image of God Must Go"

Tune: The Vicar of Bray

Now Hoyle and Russell are the thing
  And atheists the focus
Away from make-believe I'll swing
  And cease all hocus-pocus:
With Science now I will insist
  That Reason rules supreme, Sir,
Yet still maintain the Eucharist,
  Since things aren't what they seem, Sir.
Thus double-talk shall win the day
  And one and all I'll fool, which
Will let me ever preach and pray
  And still be the Bishop of Woolwich.

Song of the Bishop of Durham

I'm Jenkins, Durham is my See,
And modern is my vision:
God's thunderbolts don't frighten me —
I treat them with derision.
But Christian tenets must command
Most reverent adoration —
Which does not mean that they demand
A literal connotation.

A myth, a myth is Virgin Birth,
A myth the Resurrection!
But true it is that I am worth
My See and its direction.
Thus double-talk will win again,
My foes, I shall deter 'em,
And I will preach with might and main,
And still be the Bishop of Durham.

BET CHERRINGTON

Psalm 23a

1. MY lord is the shepherd: his mark is upon me.
2. He feedeth me with silage: he driveth me through pools of sheep-dip.
3. He sheareth the fleece from off my back: and selleth it to the spinners of wool;
4. To make fine raiment for the rich man: and for the rich man's wife, and for his daughters.
5. He selleth my children to the slaughterer: that they may furnish meat for the rich man's table.
6. He strippeth the fat from my carcase: to make candles wherewith to light the rich man's abode.
7. As for my bones, he crusheth them: to feed his dogs withal.
8. Yea, though I should stray into the wilderness of doubt: yet will he seek me out, and bear me back to his fold.
9. Surely he and his dogs will pursue me all the days of my life: and I shall dwell in captivity for ever.

DAVID OPPENHEIMER
(1914-   )

St Syphilis and All Devils

As I sit eating a Heinz Big Soup
I can hear the choir of St Syphilis and All Devils:
they are singing for me in a little chapel-of-ease,
part of the ruins of St Erysipelas-the-Less.
Big Nasties in their robes conduct the service.

The motorways are chill, and cold the concrete,
there is no nourishment in a spaghetti junction,
the foods and wines are trapped in cold tin
as everywhere the sleety rain comes down
and all the cars whizz past like lions and demons.

Unemployed boys are freezing in disaster,
the frizzy-haired girls are cold as Eskimos,
everything is packaged, disaster is packaged,
human contacts are the taunts and stabbing
dead boredom at home, outside the hellpacks. . . .

And now they unwrap the little packaged wars
lodged in their tinsel at the foot of the Christmas tree,
there are little bangs and crackers; but the big presents
remain to the last. Who will get what? All the
    choristers rise and explode in a giant crescendo. . . .

Rusted iron in broken concrete and thin dead trees.
Clear on all transistors that demonic choir
is singing enthusiastically of human breakdown,
fat fiends in surplices, St Syphilis and All Devils:
working for a profit, putting *us* in the collection.

GAVIN EWART
(1916-   )

New Approach Needed

SHOULD you revisit us,
Stay a little longer,
And get to know the place.
Experience hunger,
Madness, disease and war.
You heard about them, true,
The last time you came here;
It's different having them.
And what about a go
At love, marriage, children?
All good, but bringing some
Risk of remorse and pain
And fear of an odd sort:
A sort one should, again,
Feel, not just hear about,
To be qualified as
A human-race expert.
On local life, we trust
The resident witness,
Not the royal tourist.

People have suffered worse
And more durable wrongs
Than you did on that cross
(I know—you won't get me
Up on one of those things),
Without sure prospect of
Ascending good as new
On the third day, without
"I die, but man shall live"
As a nice cheering thought.

So, next time, come off it,
And get some service in,
Jack, long before you start
Laying down the old law:
If you still want to then.
Tell your dad that from me.

KINGSLEY AMIS
(1922-   )

Alive, Alive O

THE altar boy from a Mass for the dead
Romps through the streets of the town,
Lolls on brick studded grass
Jumps up, bolts back down
With wild pup eyes. . . .

This morning at twist of winter to spring
Small hands clutched a big brass cross
Followed the stern brow of the priest
Encircled the man in the box. . . .

A bell-tossed head sneezed
In a blue daze of incense on
Shrivelled bit lips, then
Just to stay awake, prayed
Too loud for the man to be at rest. . . .

O now where has he got to
But climbed an apple tree!

PADRIAC FIACC
(1924-   )

Some Women of Marrakesh

STRANGE as the Star in the Major Arcana,
Strange as the Queens of the Looking Glass Lands,
Women of Marrakesh dance for each other,
Snaking silk hips to the beat of their hands.

Veiled from the street, to the tower unbidden,
Free from the mosque's mathematical prayer,
In cedarwood rooms, upon white flaking balconies,
Marrakesh women meet, faces all bare.

Hidden by walls built by Sons of the Prophet,
Square walls confounding men's hard horny stare,
Circles are magicked by Marrakesh women
With swirling black brushes of gyrating hair.

Through caverns uncharted by husbands of Islam,
With passion escaping men's measuring rods,
As underground streams find a way to the rock face
Marrakesh women keep tryst with the gods.

Gods who are tumbled by Marrakesh women,
Gods who are humbled, resist if they dare
The terrible torrent the Marrakesh Goddesses
Loose as the thundering water hits the air.

Roses of Jericho, bloomed in a prison
In juices distilled in the long skirted trance,
Goddess of Rebirth, fronded from flesh dew,
Glimpsed through the Marrakesh women who dance.

Where will you go when your roots are all shattered,
How shall you go when your garden is gone,
Starkened your stems and your petals all scattered,
Torn by the concrete and seared by the sun?

Footsore for centuries, bruise eyed from weeping,
Catching the tat of the cloak she once wore,
Wrenching the lattice where daughters lie sleeping,
Banging on bolts with her knuckles beef raw,

Searching through shops, through offices, factories,
Haggard from aeons pressganged on the game,
Rouging her cheeks in bordello poxed moon glass,
Cracked throated Ceres is calling your name. . .

Somewhere in shadow awaits dark Diana,
Fledging her fury and biding her chance,
Drawing a bead on the bonds of the Goddess
Grown by the Marrakesh women who dance.

MARGARET DE V. WILLS

Quite Apart from the Holy Ghost

I REMEMBER God as an eccentric millionaire,
Locked in his workshop, beard a cloud of foggy-
                                    coloured hair,
Making the stones all different, each flower and
                                    disease,
Putting the Laps in Lapland, making China for the
                                    Chinese,
Laying down the Lake of Lucerne as smooth as
                                    blue-grey lino,
Wearily inventing the appendix and the rhino,
Making the fine fur for the mink, fine women
                                    for the fur,
Man's brain a gun, his heart a bomb, his conscience
                                    — a blur.

Christ I can see much better from here,
And Christ upon the Cross is clear.
Jesus is stretched like the skin of a kite
Over the Cross, he seems in flight
Sometimes. At times it seems more true
That he is meat nailed up alive & pain all through.
But it's hard to see Christ for priests.
That happens when
A poet engenders generations of advertising men.

ADRIAN MITCHELL
(1932-   )

The Storyteller

THEY grumbled on the way down.
"This is woman's work", said Calum,
"They know about such things."
Dougie sneezed. This was no night,
He muttered, to be away from the fire.
George clung to his lamb.
Its head nodded with each step
That he took.

The village loomed large
In the dark. "I don't know what
To say," said Calum. "I'm not
Cut out for this sort of thing."
George tightened his grip
On the lamb. It was true
What Calum said: they were all more
Familiar with this type of birth,
This soft, wet wriggling, then
The drying with handfuls of straw.

The Inn was asleep. Out back,
Past empty crates and bottles
Strewn on the court-yard
They found the stable.
The woman smiled at them.
The man fussed over her
And washed her face. George
Set down the lamb
On its unsteady legs.
Dougie said they had come
To see the baby. Calum scuffed
His feet. They looked down
At the tiny face, wrapped round
With shawl and blanket.

There was a noise at the door,
And the draught swept
Over them. A tall man
Stood in the square of darkness,
Shaking his cloak.
Out of it fell stars and swords,
Battered trumpets and candlesticks,
A fine rain of oatmeal, nails,
Rules, definitions, ifs and therefores,
Books in every language.
Joseph turned to Mary and said,
"The Storyteller has arrived."

DAVID OGSTON

The Ballad of the Blasphemy Trial

OH there is a place in Parnassus
where all the world's myths stand
rank on rank awaiting
the sign from a poet's hand.

Some are long dust and forgotten
their papyrus mummy shroud
crumbled. They wait for a scholar
to call them out of the crowd.

But some have names of thunder
that echo the centuries through
Isis, Venus, Moloch
Thor and his hammer too.

Yet at the call of a poet
each must rise and come
and only one law is god here
they must be true to their name.

So up in the morning early
Lord Jesus came to the hill
and there again he laid him down
to do the poet's will.

For love is Jesus' forename
where he sits on Parnassus hill
and he came to do his best there
as any great myth will.

And when his task was over
he went back to take his place
and all the myths moved over
and smiled into his face.

Lord Jesus he was troubled
as he gazed at the world below.
He nudged Socrates beside him
and asked was it true or no.

He saw a court and dock there
he knew them well of old
he saw what was put on trial
and the vision made him cold.

"Oh I have stood in a courtroom
and now what's this I see?
They are trying a man at the bar
and all in the name of me.

Oh I have hung between two thieves
so all my stories say
and shall the law that broke my limbs
be invoked for me today?"

Then Jesus stood on Parnassus side
and tore his long dark hair
but Socrates restrained him
and spelled it out with care.

"Although we must always follow
and be true to our stories' truth
no such constraints can bind them."
Lord Jesus gnashed his teeth.

"They have made me into a mockery
with their blasphemy of trial.
They have taken love, my given name
and broken it on a wheel.

I shall curse them in their blindness
I curse them in their pride.
They align themselves with Judas
and Pilate takes their side."

Then Socrates gave him hemlock
as they sat on Parnassus hill
to soothe his deep affliction.
"Oh do not take it ill.

We both died condemned felons
though you by another's hand
and we must forgive our children
who do not understand.

Some in the name of reason
do things I shudder for
others for love invoke you
and stand you at their bar."

But Jesus answered him fiercely
"Reason is not my name.
You must do as you have answer
I will not play their game.

I will go down to the courtyard
and hang me on a cross
while the judge pronounces sentence
and they will see their loss."

Socrates looked down sadly
and reached below his hand
to pluck the dear Lord Jesus
out of his own grandstand.

"Come up, come up, dear Jesus
they must not see you there
they will only think you demonstrate
and drag you off by your hair.

Remember your name is love, lord
come up along with me.
In time myths of love and reason
may cause the blind to see."

MAUREEN DUFFY
(1933-   )

For The Freethinker *Centenary*

THOUGHT is never free. It is bought in pain,
loneliness. Comfort clothes conformity.
Thought's a dole child, threadbare with fallibility
patched pants braced up with reason's tangled twine

is sometimes stubborn, says: "Yet it still moves,"
before the belly tucks in; is shot through
with dark tales we sucked up in childhood's pew
guilt, need, envy and rage, the wailing groves

of never-had and never-was that hang
with offerings in our family trees.
How can thought who free in this twilight sees
adrift, widdershins or we ask it be strong

to take on death, eternity, those two
sharp blades that slice poor flesh? Yet we do.

MAUREEN DUFFY

Shalom

IF there be any God
hear now the horns of Beethoven
calling heroically
in the Olympic Stadium
that building for good
shall not be brought down
by evil:
the shining plexiglass roof
of friendship
not shimmer back into myth
and disappear —
memorial to a hope of brotherhood:
the flame set high
not go out.
Hear God, if you be there,
this symphony of Beethoven
uniting the different belief
of Jew and Arab and Gentile
and speaking also for those
of no faith
desiring peace.

PATRICIA MARTLAND

God is Dead — Nietzsche

DADDY and I are always here, you know,
Whenever you want us.
We didn't like the things you said
the last time home.
Bourgeois, you said, and a word which sounded
Very like atrophied.
Daddy doesn't like the way you collect toilet graffiti.
God is dead, Nietzsche, and the reply,
Nietzsche is dead, God.

You can't expect Daddy to go round
with the plate in church
with thoughts like that in his head.
I worry too.
Structuralism sounds like a building-site,
Semiology sounds rather rude,
In a medical kind of way.
The dogs are very well, both almost human
As we've often said to you.

Please wear a vest, the days are getting
colder. We hope you will not be so rude
the next time home.
Daddy and I have just re-done your room.
The blood on the wall hardly shows
after two coats of paint.
Cambridge must be very pretty now.
I am, in spite of everything,
Your loving mother.

ELIZABETH BARTLETT
(1924-   )

Good God!

(64)

"THE ground of being" has a grand
    and philosophic ring —
but theists who would take their stand
on abstract "ground" tread shifting sand:
    it doesn't mean a thing.

(81)

If common-sense were common, no
    religions would arise:
Old Occam's razor, to and fro,
    would cut them down to size.

(76)

Why "Blessed are they who have not seen
    and yet believe"? Why should
such purblind faith the Nazarene
    extol, as something good?
And worse, he would to Hell consign
    those men who dared to doubt
the marvels of his market line —
    who tried to work things out.

(77)

A God of Love I cannot square
With Hell—not fact, nor in the air —
    nor yet with hell-on-Earth.
Less sickening, for those who care,
if naught but neutral chance be there
    to bless, or blight, our birth.

From *Good God!*
BARBARA SMOKER
(1923-   )

PART III

TIME

So many poets speak of Time, or time, and apparently it is the most important, far-reaching and solemn matter, greater than Life, more austere than Death. But what is it? I thought that by collecting some poems on Time I might learn to understand it better. But although I found it discussed in very many ways, and very cunningly and beautifully, I was none the wiser. Perhaps this is all we can expect. We are embedded in time; it is always there, but you can never put salt on its tail and catch it and hold it. In this respect Humanists are like everyone else.

However, we can learn about "Time, Real and Imaginary", as in Coleridge's "Allegory" where the swift sister, imaginary time, outruns the plodding brother, real, objective, clock time, but is still linked to him by her concern. Or we can learn to try not to hold too strongly to the past, like poor Jim Jay, who "got stuck fast in yesterday" with fatal results. We can strive to immortalise our beloved through the printed word, as many poets have, most notably Shakespeare in several of his Sonnets. Here I have chosen a less well known poem, Walter Savage Landor's "Past ruin'd Ilion Helen lives", where he commemorates his Ianthe.

Each poet brings his particular revelation, his own sense of what time is, and perhaps in the treatment of this difficult and elusive theme his or her calibre is shown most plainly.

Eternal Time, That Wastest without Waste

ETERNAL Time, that wastest without waste,
That art, and art not, diest, and livest still;
Most slow of all, and yet of greatest haste;
Both ill and good, and neither good nor ill:
How can I justly praise thee, or dispraise?
Dark are thy nights, but bright and clear thy days.

Both free and scarce, thou giv'st and taks't again;
Thy womb that all doth breed, is tomb to all;
What so by thee has life, by thee is slain;
From thee do all things rise, by thee they fall:
Constant, inconstant, moving, standing still;
Was, Is, Shall be, do thee both breed and kill.

I lose thee, while I seek to find thee out;
The farther off, the more I follow thee;
The faster hold, the greater cause of doubt;
Was, Is, I know; but *Shall* I cannot see.
All things by thee are measured; thou, by none:
All are in thee; thou, in thyself alone.

from *A Poetical Rhapsody* (1602)
A. W.

A Comparison of the Life of Man

MAN'S life is well compared to a feast,
Furnished with choice of all variety:
To it comes Time; and as a bidden guest
He sits him down, in pomp and majesty:
The threefold age of Man the waiters be.
Then with an earthen voider, made of clay,
Comes Death, and takes the table clean away.

from *Poems in Divers Humours,* (1589)
RICHARD BARNFIELD
(1574-1627)

De Sua Clepsydra

SETTING mine hour-glass for a witness by
To measure study as the time did fly:
A lingering muse possessed my thinking brain:
My mind was reaching, but in such a vein,
As if my thoughts, by thinking brought asleep
Wingless and footless, now like snails did creep.
I eyed my glass, but he so fast did run,
That e'er I had begun, the hour was done.
The creeping sands with speedy pace were flit,
Before one reason crept out of my wit.
When I stood still, I saw how time did fly:
When my wits ran, time ran more fast than I.
Stay here: I'll change the course, let study pass,
And let time study while I am the glass.
What touch ye, sands? are little mites so fleet?
Can bodies run so swift that have no feet?
And can ye tumble time so fast away?
Then farewell hours, I'll study by the day.

THOMAS BASTARD
(1566-1618)

Plutus, Cupid, and Time

. . . AS PLUTUS, to divert his care,
Walk'd forth one morn to take the air,
CUPID o'ertook his strutting pace:
Each star'd upon the stranger's face,
Till recollection set 'em right;
For each knew t'other but by sight.
After some complimental talk,
TIME met 'em, bow'd, and join'd their walk;
Their chat on various subjects ran,
But most—what each had done for man:
PLUTUS assumes a haughty air,
Just like our purse-proud fellows here.

104

Let kings, says he, let cobblers, tell
Whose gifts among mankind excel:
Consider courts: what draws their train?
Think you 'tis loyalty, or gain?
That statesman hath the strongest hold
Whose tool of politics is gold:
By that, in former reigns, 'tis said,
The knave in power hath senates led:
By that alone he sway'd debates,
Enrich'd himself, and beggar'd states.
Forego your boast: you must conclude
That's most esteem'd that's most pursu'd.
Think, too, in what a woful plight
That wretch must live whose pocket's light —
Are not his hours by want depress'd?
Penurious care corrodes his breast:
Without respect, or love, or friends,
His solitary day descends.

You might, says CUPID, doubt my parts,
My knowledge, too, in human hearts,
Should I the pow'r of gold dispute,
Which great examples might confute.
I know, when nothing else prevails,
Persuasive money seldom fails;
That beauty, too, like other wares,
Its price, as well as conscience, bears.
Then marriage, as of late profess'd,
Is but a money job at best:
Consent, compliance, may be sold;
But love's beyond the price of gold.
Smugglers there are, who, by retail,
Expose what they call love to sale.
Such bargains are an arrant cheat;
You purchase flatt'ry and deceit.
Those who true love have ever try'd,
(The common cares of life supply'd)
No wants endure, no wishes make,
But ev'ry real joy partake:
All comfort on themselves depends;
They want nor pow'r, nor wealth, nor friends.
Love then hath ev'ry bliss in store;
'Tis friendship, and 'tis something more:

Each other ev'ry wish they give;
Not to know love, is not to live.

Or love, or money, TIME reply'd,
Were men the question to decide,
Would bear the prize; on both intent,
My boon's neglected or misspent.
'Tis I who measure vital space,
And deal out years to human race:
Though little priz'd and seldom sought,
Without me love and gold are nought.
How does the miser TIME employ?
Did I e'er see him life enjoy?
By me forsook, the hoards he won
Are scatter'd by his lavish son.
By me all useful arts are gain'd;
Wealth, learning, wisdom is attain'd.
Who then would think, since such my pow'r,
That e'er I knew an idle hour?
So subtle and so swift I fly,
Love's not more fugitive than I.
Who hath not heard coquettes complain
Of days, months, years, misspent in vain?
For TIME misus'd they pine and waste,
And love's sweet pleasures never taste.
Those who direct their TIME aright,
If love or wealth their hopes excite,
In each pursuit fit hours employ'd,
And both by TIME have been enjoy'd.
How heedless then are mortals grown!
How little is their int'rest known!
In every view they ought to mind me,
For when once lost they never find me.

   He spoke. The GODS no more contest,
And his superior gift confess'd;
That TIME, when truly understood
Is the most precious earthly good.

From *Fable XIII*
JOHN GAY
(1685-1732)

Time, Real and Imaginary

An Allegory

ON the wide level of a mountain's head,
(I knew not where, but 'twas some faery place)
Their pinions, ostrich-like, for sails outspread,
Two lovely children run an endless race,
   A sister and a brother!
   This far oustripp'd the other;
Yet ever runs she with reverted face,
And looks and listens for the boy behind:
   For he, alas! is blind!
O'er rough and smooth with even step he passed,
And knows not whether he be first or last.

SAMUEL TAYLOR COLERIDGE
(1772-1834)

Whatever Happened?

AT once whatever happened starts receding.
Panting, and back on board, we line the rail
With trousers ripped, light wallets, and lips bleeding.

Yes, gone, thank God! Remembering each detail
We toss for half the night, but find next day
All's kodak-distant. Easily, then, (though pale),

"Perspective brings significance," we say,
Unhooding our photometers, and, snap!
What can't be printed can be thrown away.

Later, it's just a lattitude: the map
Points out how unavoidable it was:
"Such coastal bedding always means mishap."

Curses? The dark? Struggling? Where's the source
Of these yarns now (except in nightmares, of course)?

PHILIP LARKIN
(1922-1987)

For Passing the Time

FOR passing the time it is a very good thing
To say, Oh, how are the vegetables growing?
How are the artichokes? Are the leeks coming on?
Will there be decent parsnips when the time comes?

I expect so: nature does not deny her abundance
To those who are patient and don't expect too much;
The leaves wither, and the leaves sprout again;
It is unchangeable as change can be.

Down by the river there are events
In every season; and the river flows
In all seasons, sometimes more, sometimes less:
It is hallowed time which passes along its banks.

But for me how can the time be hallowed?
I seek no remedy in it; there can be none.
The scent of rosemary is pungent in the nostrils:
Break the lavender stem, and recorded time.

C. H. SISSON
(1914-   )

Tree Fall

THE saw rasps the morning into logs
that chart a tree's slow foundering
sinking to a barky knee, a marooned stump
island in the woven green lawn.
Its head of mermaid hair drops, jerks on a hangman
    rope
its spread arms own gallows fork the clear sky
where the young executioner swings Tarzan
through the urban jungle, silhouetted
in stark bravado every window fills
to watch, admire up there mid-July
half naked in a sudden sunburst
as the top bows to his overgrown powerdrill
we tame at home to trim the prunus

that burgeons white hopes in the Spring.
Blinded by sun moths stagger drunk with sleep
from their doomed leaf beds. Silent in the ripped air
predator thrush and blackbird let them go.
This was a false acacia, immigrant
a locust tree, John Baptist fed on
with honey for desert breakfast, native
from the New World three hundred years ago.
The tree fellers prise its spread fingers
from their grip on the earth.
I take up a slice of trunk fallen to the ground
its sunshield kept bare of other life
as the ash drips its poison onto the soil
at its feet, an invisible wall
that moats and guards it round.
My slice shows annuities: late spring, drought, flood
mapped in its rings, graphed so fine my naked eye
can't tell them round. Maybe this morning
has shipwrecked two centuries and Mozart
is playing at the inmost ring. From Cologne bridge
you can see beyond mythical Christpoint
back to when we were children of the wood spirits
and knew what we did when we cut down trees.
See that ringed jetty? Its timbers plot
where the ships tied up with oil, gods,
wine, cooking pots, the centuries before the axe.
I hold an ache, oak corn in my palm.
The earth will make it a chronometer
and I can only guess at the time it will
tick over when the lasersaw brings it down.

MAUREEN DUFFY
(1933-   )

How round the world goes

HOW round the world goes, and everything that's in it,
The tides of gold and silver ebb and flow in a minute.
From the usurer to his sons, there a current swiftly
    runs,
From the sons to queans in chief, from the gallant to
    the thief,

From the thief unto his host, from the host to
  husbandmen,
From the country to the court, and so it comes to us
  again.
How round the world goes, and everything that's in it,
The tides of gold and silver ebb and flow in a minute.

From *The Widow,*
THOMAS MIDDLETON
(1580-1627)

Time was: Time is: Time is not

TIME *was: Time is: Time is not,* runs the rune.
Hasten then. Seize that *is,* so soon begone.
As well substract the music, keep the tune!

For no "time" ever yet in storage lay,
Sun-ambered, weathered, sweet as new-mown hay,
Waiting mind's weaving—Rumpelstiltskin's way:—

Time "real"; time rare; time wildfire-fleet; time tame;
Time telepathic, out of space, and aim;
Time starry; lunatic; ice-bleached; of flame;
Dew-transient, yet immutably the same;
Meek-mild as chickweed in a window-frame;

Tardy as gathering dust in rock-hewn vault;
Fickle as moon-flake in a mirror caught
At pause on some clear gem's scarce-visible fault . . . .

And how moves Time in triple darkness hid,
Where—mummied 'neath his coffered coverlid —
Sleeps on the Pharaoh in his pyramid:
Time disincarnate—and that sharp-nosed head?

Even though suave it seem as narded oil,
Fatal to beauty it is, and yet its foil.
It is of all things mortal the indifferent soil.

Eye can scarce tell where, the whole spectrum through,
Orange with yellow fuses, green with blue;
So Time's degrees may no less diverse show,
Yet every variant be its fraction true.

From *Winged Chariot*
WALTER DE LA MARE
(1873-1956)

The Nameless Doon

WHO were the builders? question not the silence
That settles on the lake for evermore,
Save when the sea-bird screams and to the islands
The echo answers from the steep-cliffed shore.
O half-remaining ruin, in the lore
Of human life a gap shall all deplore
Beholding thee; since thou art like the dead
Found slain, no token to reveal the why,
The name, the story. Some one murdered
We know, we guess; and gazing upon thee,
And, filled by thy long silence of reply,
We guess some garnered sheaf of tragedy;—
Of tribe or nation slain so utterly
That even their ghosts are dead, and on their grave
Springeth no bloom of legend in its wildness;
And age by age weak washing round the islands
No faintest sigh of story lisps the wave.

WILLIAM LARMINIE
(1850-1899)

You Mighty Lords

YOU mighty Lords, that with respected grace
  Do at the stern of fair example stand,
And all the body of this populace
  Guide with the only turning of your hand,
Keep a right course, bear up from all disgrace,
  Observe the point of glory to our land:

Hold up disgraced knowledge from the ground,
  Keep virtue in request, give worth her due,
Let not neglect with barbarous means confound
  So fair a good to bring in night anew.
Be not, oh be not, accessory found
  Unto her death that must give life to you.

Where will you have your virtuous names safe laid:
  In gorgeous tombs, in sacred cells secure?
Do you not see those prostrate heaps betrayed
  Your fathers' bones, and could not keep them sure?
And will you trust deceitful stones fair laid,
  And think they will be to your honour truer?

No, no, unsparing time will proudly send
  A warrant unto wrath that with one frown
Will all these mock'ries of vainglory rend,
  And make them as before, ungraced, unknown,
Poor idle honours that can ill defend
  Your memories, that cannot keep their own.

And whereto serve that wondrous *trophei* now,
  That on the goodly plain near Wilton stands?
That huge dumb heap, that cannot tell us how,
  Nor what, nor whence it was, nor with whose hands,
Nor for whose glory, it was set to show
  How much our pride mocks that of other lands?

Whereon, whenas the gazing passenger
  Hath looked with greedy admiration,
And fain would know his birth, and what he were,
  How there erected, and how long agone,
Enquires, and asks his fellow traveller,
  What he hath heard, and his opinion:

And he knows nothing. Then he turns again,
    And looks, and sighs, and then admires afresh,
And in himself with sorrow doth complain
    The misery of dark forgetfulness;
Angry with time that nothing should remain
    Our greatest wonders-wonder to express.

SAMUEL DANIEL
(1562-1619)

Mutability

WE are as clouds that veil the midnight moon;
    How restlessly they speed, and gleam, and quiver,
Streaking the darkness radiantly!—yet soon
    Night closes round, and they are lost for ever:

Or like forgotten lyres, whose dissonant strings
    Give various response to each varying blast,
To whose frail frame no second motion brings
    One mood or modulation like the last.

We rest.—A dream has power to poison sleep;
    We rise.—One wandering thought pollutes the day;
We feel, conceive or reason, laugh or weep;
    Embrace fond woe, or cast our cares away:

It is the same!—For, be it joy or sorrow,
    The path of its departure still is free:
Man's yesterday may ne'er be like his morrow;
    Naught may endure but Mutability.

PERCY BYSSHE SHELLEY
(1792-1822)

The Mahratta Ghats

THE valleys crack and burn, the exhausted plains
Sink their black teeth into the horny veins
Straggling the hills' red thighs, the bleating goats
— Dry bents and bitter thistles in their throats —
Thread the loose rocks by immemorial tracks.
Dark peasants drag the sun upon their backs.

High on the ghat the new turned soil is red.
The sun has ground it to the finest red,
It lies like gold within each horny hand.
Siva has split his seed upon this land.

Will she who burns and withers on the plain
Leave, ere too late, her scraggy herds of pain,
The cow-dung fire and the trembling beasts,
The little wicked gods, the grinning priests,
And climb, before a thousand years have fled,
High as the eagle to her mountain bed
Whose soil is fine as flour and blood-red?
But no! She cannot move. Each arid patch
Owns the lean folk who plough and scythe and thatch
Its grudging yield and scratch its stubborn stones.
The small gods suck the marrow from their bones.

Who is it climbs the summit of the road?
Only the beggar bumming his dark load.
Who was it cried to see the falling star?
Only the landless soldier lost in war.

And did a thousand years go by in vain?
And does another thousand start again?

ALUN LEWIS
(1915-1944)

January in Plainfield

OUR old wind crosses the tame border,
The only immigrant we never stop to question.
All the years I haven't felt it through my coat
It has still whistled little taunts under Indiana doors.
Now I meet this wind again with crepe on its hat.
When she was alive
Only last week this snow was falling,
Live snow, grey strands in a white-haired sky.
Now it lies in rigid lumps, a growth on the sidewalk.
She is a memory in a thousand minds,
And careful, I look both ways, proceed with caution,
To protect the fragile part of her that has to last my life.

SARAH LAWSON
(1943-   )

Let Others Sing of Knights and Paladins

LET others sing of knights and paladins
In aged accents and untimely words;
Paint shadows in imaginary lines,
Which well the reach of their high wits records:
But I must sing of thee, and those fair eyes
Authentic shall my verse in time to come;
When yet th'unborn shall say, "Lo where she lies,
Whose beauty made him speak that else was dumb."
These are the arks, the trophies I erect,
That fortify thy name against old age;
And these thy sacred virtues must protect
Against the dark, and time's consuming rage.
    Though th'error of my youth in them appear,
    Suffice they show I lived and loved thee dear.

from *Sonnets to Delia*
SAMUEL DANIEL
(1562-1619)

Past Ruin'd Ilion Helen Lives

PAST ruin'd Ilion Helen lives,
    Alcestis rises from the shades;
Verse calls them forth; 'tis verse that gives
    Immortal youth to mortal maids.

Soon shall Oblivion's deepening veil
    Hide all the peopled hills you see,
The gay, the proud, while lovers hail
    These many summers you and me.

The tear for fading beauty check,
    For passing glory cease to sigh;
One form shall rise above the wreck,
    One name, Ianthe, shall not die.

WALTER SAVAGE LANDOR
(1775-1864)

Prologue*

THE charms of silence through this square be thrown,
That an un-used attention (like a jewel)
May hang at every ear, for we present
Matter above the vulgar argument:
Yet drawn so lively, that the weakest eye,
(Through those thin veils we hang between your sight
And this our piece) may reach the mystery:
What in it is most grave, will most delight.
But as in landskip, towns and woods appear
Small afar off, yet to the optic sense,
The mind shows them as great as those more near;
So, winged Time that long ago flew hence
You must fetch back, with all those golden years
He stole, and here imagine still he stands,
Thrusting his silver lock into your hands.
There hold it but two hours—it shall from graves
Raise up the dead; upon this narrow floor
Swell up an ocean (with an armed fleet),
And lay the dragon at a dove's soft feet.

These wonders sit and see, sending as guides
Your judgement, not your passions: passion slides,
While judgement goes upright: for though the Muse
(That's thus inspired) a novel path does tread,
She's free from foolish boldness, or base dread.
Lo, scorn she scorns, and Envy's rankling tooth,
For this is all she does—she wakens Truth.

From *The Whore of Babylon*
THOMAS DEKKER
(1570-1638)

*The actor introduces the play.

Shadows

ARE they shadows that we see,
And can shadows pleasures give?
Pleasures only shadows be,
Cast by bodies we conceive;
  And are made the things we deem
  In those figures which they seem.

But these pleasures vanish fast,
Which by shadows are expressed:
Pleasures are not, if they last;
In their passing is the best.
  Glory is most bright and gay
  In a flash, and so away.

Feed apace then, greedy eyes,
On the wonder you behold;
Take it sudden as it flies,
Though you take it not to hold:
  When your eyes have done their part,
  Thought must lengthen it in the heart.

From *Tethys' Festival*
SAMUEL DANIEL
(1562-1619)

Jim Jay

Do diddle di do,
  Poor Jim Jay
Got stuck fast
  In Yesterday.
Squinting he was,
  On cross-legs bent,
Never heeding
  The wind was spent.
Round veered the weathercock,
  The sun drew in —
And stuck was Jim
  Like a rusty pin. . . .
We pulled and we pulled
  From seven till twelve,
Jim, too frightened
  To help himself.
But all in vain.
  The clock struck one,
And there was Jim
  A little bit gone.
At half-past five
  You scarce could see
A glimpse of his flapping
  Handkerchee.
And when came noon,
  And we climbed sky-high,
Jim was a speck
  Slip-slipping by.
Come to-morrow,
  The neighbours say,
He'll be past crying for;
  Poor Jim Jay.

WALTER DE LA MARE
(1873-1956)

From far, from eve and morning

XXXII

FROM far, from eve and morning
    And yon twelve-winded sky,
The stuff of life to knit me
    Blew hither: here am I.

Now—for a breath I tarry
    Nor yet disperse apart—
Take my hand quick and tell me,
    What have you in your heart.

Speak now, and I will answer;
    How shall I help you, say;
Ere to the wind's twelve quarters
    I take my endless way.

from *A Shropshire Lad*
A. E. HOUSMAN
(1859-1936)

To the Virgins, to Make Much of Time

GATHER ye rosebuds while ye may,
Old Time is still a-flying:
And this same flower that smiles today
Tomorrow will be dying.

The glorious Lamp of Heaven, the Sun,
The higher he's a-getting,
The sooner will his race be run,
And nearer he's to setting.

That age is best which is the first,
When youth and blood are warmer;
But being spent, the worse, and worst
Times still succeed the former.

Then be not coy, but use your time,
And while ye may, go marry:
For having lost but once your prime,
You may for ever tarry.

ROBERT HERRICK
(1591-1674)

Now is a Moveable Feast

WE must not forget that Now is a moveable feast.
There was a Now once when hearts were heavy in
Sparta
And many men of many empires have feared, and
laughter
Has died on lips that are now skulls. But they were
released.
Think of all those black Nows of the human pain
And the mad and merciless who made them.
Napoleon made heavy hearts, but Time unweighed
them,
And Wars of Roses and Royalists have sunk into peace
again.
There must have been lovers under Cromwell who
thought,
All at an end! Must have been poets who could not see
beyond Bosworth Field.
Well then. They are History now. Please God, we too
may be taught
As History in another Now—all safe, secret and sealed.

T. H. WHITE
(1906-1964)

To-day

ALONE To-day stands in the sun,
Why dream they who that race must run?

Between two precipices steep
To-day arises from the deep.

Athwart the deep abyss of night
It stretches like a ribbon bright.

Between the dawn and dusk it lies,
Apex of two eternities.

To-morrow dim and Yesterday
Are lost within that twilight grey.

Only a slender path of light
Between the double jaws of night.

While the full glory of the sun
Proclaims To-day the only one.

EVEREST LEWIN

Cities and Thrones and Powers

CITIES and Thrones and Powers
    Stand in Time's eye,
Almost as long as flowers,
    Which daily die:
But, as new buds put forth
    To glad new men,
Out of the spent and unconsidered Earth
    The Cities rise again.

This season's Daffodil,
    She never hears
What change, what chance, what chill,
    Cut down last year's;
But with bold countenance,
    And knowledge small,
Esteems her seven days' continuance
    To be perpetual.

So Time that is o'er-kind
    To all that be,
Ordains us e'en as blind,
    As bold as she:
That in our very death,
    And burial sure,
Shadow to shadow, well persuaded, saith,
    "See how our works endure!"

RUDYARD KIPLING
(1865-1936)

PART IV

HUMANITY IN NATURE

The first poems here are about animals, birds, insects and fish, related to the human being by comparison or allusion. Robert Frost in "Departmental" finds ant behaviour not "ungentle. But thoroughly departmental". Leigh Hunt gives us man's view of a fish, then the fishy view of man. John Montague in "The Trout" vividly conveys the trout's terror on realising that he is caught.

I have found no firm-dividing line between the human animal and other creatures, and I have gathered these poems to exemplify our close bonds with nature. I was solitary as a child, and free to wander in fields and woods. I found that most adults were both ignorant and scornful of wild life. But I had seen that birds and animals show emotions much like ours, though they do not always communicate them in signals which we can recognise.

T. H. White's "Stuffed Pheasant" brings us up with a jerk. This bird, and the humans who have stuffed him, are ridiculous. We cannot any longer ride dreamily with nature, observing and commenting. We move into larger and more challenging themes. Did Napoleon succumb to winter or did he project his own bleak nature on to History? Which is master, the "Sun Rising" or the strong lovers who together create the life of the world? Will the loving mother be able to hold her darling daughter against the pull of the sea? The Nature entangling us is more than flora and fauna: it is the sea, the earth, sun, moon and stars, chemistry and physics—and if we misunderstand it we shall burn more than our fingers.

Barbara Smoker robustly states, "We're social—and survive", but Pat Arrowsmith takes a more wary stance. Her two poems, which end this section, show us the microcosm of the Rock Pool, unpolluted and intact in its beauty. "Greenhouse", a larger place, is our own heedless and vulnerable world, the global village which we can quickly and permanently damage or destroy. It is time we woke up and took action to prevent rapid deterioration and to maintain the equilibrium between man and nature.

Departmental

AN ant on the tablecloth
Ran into a dormant moth
Of many times his size.
He showed not the least surprise.
His business wasn't with such.
He gave it scarcely a touch,
And was off on his duty run.
Yet if he encountered one
Of the hive's inquiry squad
Whose work is to find out God
And the nature of time and space,
He would put him onto the case.
Ants are a curious race;
One crossing with hurried tread
The body of one of their dead
Isn't given a moment's arrest —
Seems not even impressed.
But he no doubt reports to any
With whom he crosses antennae,
And they no doubt report
To the higher up at court.
Then the word goes out in Formic:
"Death's come to Jerry McCormic,
Our selfless forager Jerry.
Will the special Janizary
Whose office it is to bury
The dead of the commissary
Go bring him home to his people.
Lay him in state on a sepal.
Wrap him for shroud in a petal.
Embalm him with ichor of nettle.
This is the word of your Queen."
And presently on the scene
Appears a solemn mortician;
And taking formal position
With feelers calmly atwiddle,
Seizes the dead by the middle,
And heaving him high in the air,
Carries him out of there.
No one stands round to stare.
It is nobody else's affair.

It couldn't be called ungentle.
But how thoroughly departmental.

ROBERT FROST
(1874-1963)

To Be Called a Bear

BEARS gash the forest trees
    To mark the bounds
    Of their own hunting grounds;
They follow the wild bees
    Point by point home
    For love of honeycomb;
They browse on blueberries.

Then should I stare
If I am called a bear,
And is it not the truth?
Unkempt and surly with a sweet tooth
I tilt my muzzle toward the starry hub
Where Queen Callisto guards her cub,

But envy those that here
    All winter breathing slow
    Sleep warm under the snow,
That yawn awake when the skies clear,
    And lank with longing grow
No more than one brief month a year.

ROBERT GRAVES
(1895-1985)

To a Mouse,
On Turning Her Up in Her Nest, With the
Plough, November 1785

WEE, sleekit, cowrin, tim'rous beastie,
O, what a panic's in thy breastie!
Thou need na start awa sae hasty,   hurrying
   Wi' bickering brattle! scamper
I wad be laith to rin an' chase thee,   loath
   Wi' murd'ring pattle!   plough-staff

I'm truly sorry Man's dominion
Has broken Nature's social union,
An' justifies that ill opinion,
   Which makes thee startle,
At me, thy poor, earth-born companion,
   An' fellow-mortal!

I doubt na, whyles, but thou may thieve;   sometimes
What then? poor beastie, thou maun live!
A daimen icker in a thrave   odd ear
   'S a sma' request. twenty-four
I'll get a blessin wi' the lave,   sheaves
   An' never miss't!   what's left

Thy wee-bit housie, too, in ruin!
It's silly wa's the win's are strewin!   feeble
An' naething, now, to big a new ane,   build
   O' foggage green!   moss
An' bleak December's winds ensuin,
   Baith snell an' keen!   biting

Thou saw the fields laid bare an' waste,
An' weary Winter comin fast,
An' cozie heare, beneath the blast,
   Thou thought to dwell,
Till crash! the cruel coulter past
   Out thro' thy cell.

That wee-bit heap o' leaves an' stibble   stubble
Has cost thee monie a weary nibble!
Now thou's turn'd out, for a' thy trouble,
    But house or hald,   holding
To thole the Winter's sleety dribble,   endure
    An' cranreuch cauld!   hoar-frost

But, Mousie, thou art no thy lane,   alone
In proving foresight may be vain:
The best-laid schemes o' Mice an' Men
    Gang aft a-gley,   awry
An' lea'e us nought but grief an' pain,
    For promis'd joy!

Still thou art blest, compar'd wi' me!
The present only toucheth thee:
But, Och! I backward cast my e'e
    On prospects drear!
An' forward, tho' I canna see,
    I guess an' fear!

ROBERT BURNS
(1759-1796)

A Riddle

HERE lies one who never drew
Blood himself, yet many slew;
Gave the gun its aim, and figure
Made in field, yet ne'er pulled trigger;
Armed men have gladly made
Him their guide, and him obeyed;
At his signified desire
Would advance, present, and fire —
Stout he was, and large of limb,
Scores have fled in spite of him:
And to all this fame he rose,
Only following his nose.
Neptune was he called; not he
Who controls the boist'rous sea,
But of happier command,
Neptune of the furrowed land;
And, your wonder vain to shorten,
Pointer to Sir John Throckmorton.

WILLIAM COWPER
(1731-1800)

The Maldive Shark

ABOUT the Shark, phlegmatical one,
Pale sot of the Maldive sea,
The sleek little pilot-fish, azure and slim,
How alert in attendance be.
From his saw-pit of mouth, from his charnel of maw
They have nothing of harm to dread,
But liquidly glide on his ghastly flank
Or before his Gorgonian head;
Or lurk in the port of serrated teeth
In white triple tiers of glittering gates,
And there find a haven when peril's abroad,
An asylum in jaws of the Fates!
They are friends; and friendly they guide him to prey,
Yet never partake of the treat—
Eyes and brains to the dotard lethargic and dull,
Pale ravener of horrible meat.

HERMAN MELVILLE
(1819-91)

The Grey Squirrel

LIKE a small grey
coffee-pot,
sits the squirrel.
He is not

all he should be,
kills by dozens
trees, and eats
his red-brown cousins.

The keeper on the
other hand,
who shot him, is
a Christian, and

loves his enemies.
Which shows
the squirrel was not
one of those.

HUMBERT WOLFE
(1885-1940)

The Mad Yak

I AM watching them churn the last milk
   they'll ever get from me.
They are waiting for me to die;
They want to make buttons out of my bones.
Where are my sisters and brothers?
That tall monk there, loading my uncle,
   he has a new cap.
And that idiot student of his —
   I never saw that muffler before.
Poor uncle, he lets them load him.
How sad he is, how tired!
I wonder what they'll do with his bones?
And that beautiful tail!
How many shoelaces will they make of that!

GREGORY CORSO
(1930-   )

To My Tortoise Ananke

SAY it were true that thou outliv'st us all,
  O footstool once of Venus; come, renew
  Thy tale of old Greek isles, where thy youth grew
In myrtle shadow, near her temple wall;

Or tell me how the eagle let thee fall
  Upon the Greek bard's head from heaven's blue,
  And Apathy killed Song. And is it true
That thy domed shell would bear a huge stone ball?

O Tortoise, Tortoise, there are weights, alack!
  Heavier than stone, and viewless as the air,
Which none have ever tried upon thy back;

Which, ever and anon, we men must bear —
  Weights which would make thy solid cover crack
And how we bear them, let those ask who care.

EUGENE LEE-HAMILTON
(1845-1907)

Mosquito

WHEN did you start your tricks
Monsieur?

What do you stand on such high legs for?
Why this length of shredded shank
You exaltation?

Is it that you shall lift your centre of gravity upwards
And weigh no more than air as you alight upon me,
Stand upon me weightless, you phantom?

I heard a woman call you the Winged Victory
In sluggish Venice.
You turn your head towards your tail, and smile.

How can you put so much devilry
Into that translucent phantom shred
Of frail corpus?

Queer, with your thin wings and your streaming legs
How you sail like a heron, or a dull clot of air,
A nothingness.

Yet what an aura surrounds you;
Your evil little aura, prowling, and casting a numbness
   on my mind.

That is your trick, your bit of filthy magic:
Invisibility, and the anaesthetic power
To deaden my attention in your direction.

But I know your game now, streaky sorcerer.

Queer, how you stalk and prowl the air
In circles and evasions, enveloping me,
Ghoul on wings
Winged Victory.

Settle, and stand on long thin shanks
Eyeing me sideways, and cunningly conscious that I
am aware,
You speck.

I hate the way you lurch off sideways into air
Having read my thoughts against you.

Come then, let us play at unawares,
And see who wins in this sly game of bluff.
Man or mosquito.

You don't know that I exist, and I don't know that you
   exist.

Now then!

It is your trump
It is your hateful little trump
You pointed fiend,
Which shakes my sudden blood to hatred of you:
It is your small, high, hateful bugle in my ear.

Why do you do it?
Surely it is bad policy.

They say you can't help it.

If that is so, then I believe a little in Providence
    protecting the innocent.
But it sounds so amazingly like a slogan
A yell of triumph as you snatch my scalp.

Blood, red blood
Super-magical
Forbidden liquor.

I behold you stand
For a second enspasmed in oblivion,
Obscenely ecstasied
Sucking live blood,
My blood.

Such silence, such suspended transport,
Such gorging,
Such obscenity of trespass.

You stagger
As well as you may.
Only your accursed hairy frailty
Your own imponderable weightlessness
Saves you, wafts you away on the very draught my
    anger makes in its snatching.

Away with a paean of derision
You winged blood-drop.

Can I not overtake you?
Are you one too many for me,
Winged Victory?
Am I not mosquito enough to out-mosquito you?

Queer, what a big stain my sucked blood makes
Beside the infinitesimal faint smear of you!
Queer, what a dim dark smudge you have disappeared
    into!

D. H. LAWRENCE
(1885-1930)

Calyptorhynchus Funereus

ONE wan bird walks close to the mesh of the aviary,
As though taking pleasure
In my company.

On perches behind him brilliant birds balance and
    flicker
To preen each flamboyant,
Erratic feather.

Clumsily this bird walks near my prohibited hand.
Draggles one cloudy wing
To stand

Rebuking endearments with a hoarse, broken cry.
I probe for a cause
The inert depths of his eye.

Nothing but light reflected: no sign of pain nor fear.
One horny yellow claw
Grips the upright bar.

But as though tear-weighted, his eyelid falls, downcast.
Despairingly a feather
Drifts to the dust.

Without words I can do nothing he wants me to do.
Useless, I stroke his claw
Unwilling to go.

He cries out desperately, as though for release
From where he is blackly trapped
In a feathered hearse.

His hieroglyph my mind cannot resolve, nor read,
Only a finger through the mesh
Can brush his head

To caress the body of his grave incomprehension
With amity, with amity,
Again and again.

ZOE BAILEY
(1930-   )

133

To a Fish

You strange, astonished-looking, angel-faced,
  Dreary-mouthed, gaping wretches of the sea,
  Gulping salt water everlastingly,
Cold-blooded, though with red your blood be graced,
And mute, though dwellers in the roaring waste;
  And you, all shapes beside, that fishy be, —
  Some round, some flat, some long, all devilry,
Legless, unloving, infamously chaste: —

O scaly, slippery, wet, swift, staring wights,
  What is't ye do? What life lead? Eh, dull goggles?
How do ye vary your vile days and nights?
  How pass your Sundays? Are ye still but joggles
In ceaseless wash? Still nought but gapes, and bites,
  And drinks, and stares, diversified with boggles?

A Fish Answers

Amazing monster! that, for ought I know,
  With the first sight of thee didst make our race
  For ever stare! O flat and shocking face,
Grimly divided from the breast below!
Thou that on dry land horribly dost go
  With a split body and most ridiculous pace,
  Prong after prong, disgracer of all grace,
Long-useless-finned, haired, upright, unwet, slow!

O breather of unbreathable, sword-sharp air,
  How canst exist? How bear thyself, thou dry
And dreary sloth? What particle canst share
  Of the only blessed life, the watery?
I sometimes see of ye an actual *pair*
  Go by! linked fin by fin! most odiously.

From *The Fish, the Man, and the Spirit*
HENRY LEIGH HUNT
(1784-1859)

The Rivals

I HEARD a bird at dawn
Singing sweetly on a tree,
That the dew was on the lawn,
And the wind was on the lea;
But I didn't listen to him,
For he didn't sing to me!

I didn't listen to him,
For he didn't sing to me
That the dew was on the lawn,
And the wind was on the lea!
I was singing at the time,
Just as prettily as he!

I was singing all the time,
Just as prettily as he,
About the dew upon the lawn,
And the wind upon the lea:
So I didn't listen to him,
As he sang upon a tree!

JAMES STEPHENS
(1882-1950)

The Trout

FLAT on the bank I parted
Rushes to ease my hands
In the water without ripple
And tilt them slowly downstream
To where he lay, light as a leaf,
In his fluid sensual dream.

Bodiless lord of creation
I hung briefly above him
Savouring my own absence
Senses expanding in the slow
Motion, the photographic calm
That grows before action.

As the curve of my hands
Swung under his body
He surged, with visible pleasure.
I was so preternaturally close
I could count every stipple
But still cast no shadow, until

The two palms crossed in a cage
Under the lightly pulsing gills.
Then (entering my own enlarged
Shape, which rode on the water)
I gripped. To this day I can
Taste his terror on my hands.

JOHN MONTAGUE
(1929-   )

In Midst of Woods or Pleasant Grove

IN midst of woods or pleasant grove
    Where all sweet birds do sing,
Methought I heard so rare a sound,
    Which made the heavens to ring.
The charm was good, the noise full sweet,
    Each bird did play his part;
And I admired to hear the same;
    Joy sprung into my heart.

The blackbird made the sweetest sound,
    Whose tunes did far excel,
Full pleasantly and most profound
    Was all things placed well.
Thy pretty tunes, mine own sweet bird,
    Done with so good a grace,
Extols thy name, prefers the same,
    Abroad in every place.

Thy music grave, bedecked well
With sundry points of skill,
Bewrays thy knowledge excellent,
Engrafted in thy will.
My tongue shall speak, my pen shall write,
In praise of thee to tell.
The sweetest bird that ever was,
In friendly sort, farewell.

From *Songs and Psalms*, John Mundy (1594)
ANON

The Stuffed Pheasant

THE Romans were never in Erin. Their plethoric bird,
The pheasant who falls to the pop of the English earl
Is a rarity with us. His clutter seldom is heard.
But in our best room, in a bower of mother of pearl
Printed "Present from Cork", and of pampas grass
  placed in pink pots,
Proudly upon the piano the pheasant is seen.
He is perched on a boulder of papier-mache done
  green.
He is spurred, he is plumed, he is dusty, and
  gorgeously rots.
He stretches his tail to the moths and his orgulous
  bosom though dead
To the paraffin lamp. He wobbles a little if I
Tread on the loose board. He does not remember the
  sky.
The person who stuffed him has given him horns on
  his head,
Like the Long-eared Owl, and I also, I do not
  remember
Whether he had horns or not—as he flew and he
  floated on high,
Dustless, displaying and dreading to die,
Grand in his gold mail, a living, a light-giving ember
Refulgent from the red wood to this undreamed of rath
  on the piano
Some long-ago December.

T. H. WHITE
(1906-1964)

Napoleon

"WHAT is the world, O soldiers?
It is I:
I, this incessant snow,
This northern sky;
Soldiers, this solitude
Through which we go
Is I."

WALTER DE LA MARE
(1873-1956)

Wilderness

THERE is a wolf in me. . . fangs pointed for tearing
 gashes. . .
 a red tongue for raw meat. . . and the hot lapping
 of
 blood—I keep this wolf because the wilderness gave
 it to
 me and the wilderness will not let it go.

There is a fox in me. . . a silver-gray fox. . . I sniff
 and
 guess. . . I pick things out of the wind and air. . . I
 nose in
 the dark night and take sleepers and eat them and
 hide the
 feathers. . . I circle and loop and double-cross.

There is a hog in me. . . a snout and a belly. . . a
 machinery
 for eating and grunting. . . a machinery for sleeping
 satisfied in the sun—I got this too from the
 wilderness and
 the wilderness will not let it go.

There is a fish in me. . . I know I came from
    salt-blue
    water-gates. . . I scurried with shoals of herring . . I
    blew
    waterspouts with porpoises. . . before land was. . .
    before
    the water went down. . . before Noah. . . before the
    first
    chapter of Genesis.

There is a baboon in me. . . clambering-clawed. . .
    dog-faced. . . yawping a galoot's* hunger. . . hairy
    under
    the armpits. . . here are the hawk-eyed hankering
    men.
    here are the blond and blue-eyed women. . . here
    they
    hide curled asleep waiting. . . ready to snarl and
    kill. . .
    ready to sing and give milk. . . waiting—I keep the
    baboon because the wilderness says so.

There is an eagle in me and a mockingbird. . . and
    the eagle
    flies among the Rocky Mountains of my dreams and
    fights among the Sierra crags of what I want. . . and
    the
    mockingbird warbles in the early forenoon before the
    dew
    is gone, warbles in the underbrush of my
    Chattanoogas
    of hope, gushes over the blue Ozark foothills of my
    wishes—And I got the eagle and the mockingbird
    from the wilderness.

O, I got a zoo, I got a menagerie, inside my ribs,
    under my
bony head, under my red-valve heart—and I got
    something
else: it is a man-child heart, a woman-child heart: it
    is a
father and mother and lover: it came from
    God-Knows-
Where: it is going to God-Knows-Where—For I am
    the
keeper of the zoo: I say yes and no: I sing and kill
    and
work: I am a pal of the world. I came from the
    wilderness.

CARL SANDBURG
(1878-1967)

*rough lout

Spring

WHEN daisies pied and violets blue
    And lady-smocks all silver-white
And cuckoo-buds of yellow hue
    Do paint the meadows with delight,
The cuckoo then, on every tree,
Mocks married men; for thus sings he,
    Cuckoo;
    Cuckoo, cuckoo: O word of fear,
    Unpleasing to a married ear!

When shepherds pipe on oaten straws
    And merry larks are ploughmen's clocks,
When turtles tread, and rooks, and daws,
    And maidens bleach their summer smocks,
The cuckoo then, on every tree,
Mocks married men; for thus sings he,
    Cuckoo;
    Cuckoo, cuckoo: O word of fear,
    Unpleasing to a married ear!

Winter

WHEN icicles hang by the wall,
  And Dick the shepherd blows his nail,
And Tom bears logs into the hall,
  And milk comes frozen home in pail;
When blood is nipp'd, and ways be foul,
Then nightly sings the staring owl
  Tu-whit,
Tu-who, a merry note,
While greasy Joan doth keel the pot.

When all aloud the wind doth blow,
  And coughing drowns the parson's saw,
And birds sit brooding in the snow,
  And Marian's nose looks red and raw;
When roasted crabs hiss in the bowl,
Then nightly sings the staring owl
  Tu-whit,
Tu-who, a merry note,
While greasy Joan doth keel the pot.

From *Love's Labour Lost*
WILLIAM SHAKESPEARE
(1564-1616)

Growing, flying, happening

SAY the soft bird's name, but do not be surprised
to see it fall
headlong, struck skyless, into its pigeonhole —
columba palumbus and you have it dead,
wedged, neat, unwinged in your head.

That that black-backed tatter-winged thing
straking the harbour water and then plummeting
down, to come up, sleek head-a-cock,
a minted herring shining in its beak,
is a *guillemot*, is neither here nor there
in the amazement of its rising,
wings slicing the stiff salt air.

That of that spindling spear-leaved plant,
wearing the palest purple umbel,
many-headed, blue-tinted, stilt-stalked
at the stream-edge, one should say briefly
angelica, is by-the-way (though grant
the name itself to be beautiful).
Grant too that any name
makes its own music, that *bryony, sally-my-handsome*
burst at their sound into flower,
and that *falcon* and *phalarope* fly off in the ear,
still,
names are for saying at home.

The point is seeing—the grace
beyond recognition, the ways
of the bird rising, unnamed, unknown,
beyond the range of language, beyond its noun.
Eyes open on growing, flying, happening,
and go on opening. Manifold, the world
dawns on unrecognising, realising eyes.
Amazement is the thing.
Not love, but the astonishment of loving.

ALASTAIR REID

Weeds

SOME people are flower lovers.
I'm a weed lover.

Weeds don't need planting in well-drained soil;
They don't ask for fertilizer or bits of rag to scare
    away birds
They come without invitation;
And they don't take the hint when you want them to go.
Weeds are nobody's guests:
More like squatters.

Coltsfoot laying claim to every-new-dug clump of clay;
Pearlwort scraping up a living from a ha'porth of
    mortar;
Dandelions you daren't pick or you know what will
    happen;
Sour docks that make a first-rate poultice for nettle-
    stings;
And flat-foot plantain in the back street,
    gathering more dust than the dustmen.

Even the names are a folk-song:
Fat hen, rat's tail, cat's ear, old men's baccy and
    Stinking Billy
Ring a prettier chime for me than honeysuckle or
    jasmine,
And Sweet Cicely smells cleaner than Sweet William
    though
    she's barred from the garden.

And they have their uses, weeds.
Think of the old, worked-out mines —
Quarries and tunnels, earth scorched and scruffy,
    torn-up railways, splintered sleepers,
And a whole Sahara of grit and smother and cinders.

But go in summer and where is all the clutter?
For a new town has risen of a thousand towers,
Sparkling like granite, swaying like larches,
And every spiky belfry humming with a peal of bees.
Rosebay willowherb:
Only a weed!

Flowers are for wrapping in cellophane to present as a
    bouquet;
Flowers are for prize-arrangements in vases and silver
    tea-pots;
Flowers are for plaiting into funeral wreaths.
You can keep your flowers.
Give me weeds!

                              NORMAN NICHOLSON
                              (1914-   )

Putting in the Seed

YOU come to fetch me from my work tonight
When supper's on the table, and we'll see
If I can leave off burying the white
Soft petals fallen from the apple-tree
(Soft petals, yes, but not so barren quite,
Mingled with these, smooth bean and wrinkled pea;)
And go along with you ere you lose sight
Of what you came for and become like me,
Slave to a springtime passion for the earth.
How Love burns through the Putting in the Seed
On through the watching for that early birth
When, just as the soil tarnished with weed,
The sturdy seedling with arched body comes
Shouldering its way and shedding the earth crumbs.

ROBERT FROST
(1874-1963)

Tell Me, Tell Me, Sarah Jane

TELL me, tell me, Sarah Jane,
    Tell me, dearest daughter,
Why are you holding in your hand
    A thimbleful of water?
Why do you hold it to your eye
    And gaze both late and soon
From early morning light until
    The rising of the moon?

Mother, I hear the mermaids cry,
    I hear the mermen sing,
And I can see the sailing-ships
    All made of sticks and string.
And I can see the jumping fish,
    The whales that fall and rise
And swim about the waterspout
    That swarms up to the skies.

Tell me, tell me, Sarah Jane,
  Tell your darling mother,
Why do you walk beside the tide
  As though you loved none other?
Why do you listen to a shell
  And watch the billows curl,
And throw away your diamond ring
  And wear instead the pearl?

Mother I hear the water
  Beneath the headland pinned,
And I can see the sea-gull
  Sliding down the wind.
I taste the salt upon my tongue
  As sweet as sweet can be.

Tell me, my dear, whose voice you hear?

It is the sea, the sea.

CHARLES CAUSLEY
(1917-   )

Man About to Enter Sea

WALKING into the summer cold sea
                    arms folded
trying to keep the wave and frolicy bather
splashings from further chilling him
He moves as if not to—but I know
he'll eventually go with a NOW IN! and
become warm —

That curious warm is all too familiar
as when frogs from fish kicked
and fins winged flew
and, whatever it was decided lungs
and a chance in the change above the sea —

There he wades millions of years that are legs
back into that biggest and strangest of wombs
He stands—the sea is up to his belly button
— He would it was nothing more than a holiday's dip

But I feel he's algae for skin
He who calls the dinosaur his unfortunate brother
And what with crawling anthropods
oh they're only bathers on a summer shore
yet it is possible to drown in a surface of air
deem the entire earth one NOW IN! and once in
fated out again —

GREGORY CORSO
(1930-   )

Surfers

COUCHED in a recess from the wind I've seen
ravens fly back and forth to this cliff-ledge,
and watched the sea returning, and its sheen

turn bluebottle-blue flecked with indigo,
as though ink dropped into an abalone
accounted for that darkening. The flow

is rapid, and surf blazes across flats
burnished a hard gold by the wind, ribbed sand
planed level as a sheet of glass. In hats

and beach shorts, the surfing crowd congregate
beneath the sea wall, and out of the wind,
absorb the sun's fierce energies, the slate-

like textures of their bodies oiled to bear
both sea and sun. Up here I watch those birds
drop down through a blue crystal of sea air

and comb beached drifts of wrack dried by the heat
to fossil strands where flies fester. Each wave
asserts a resonance—a drumming beat

communicated to the group who tan,
awaiting a heavier lift of surf
to call them to their boards. I watch a man

squat down, his pulse picking up the rhythm
of each new smoking wall of surf that gains
momentum, shot through with light by the sun

to subside with a mulling poker's hiss.
He's like a sentry in his black peaked cap,
maintaining vigil, and at his raised fist

the word is out, and down the beach they race
these tiny figures running with their boards
into the wind and the blue rim of space.

JEREMY REED

The Sun Rising

BUSY old fool, unruly Sun,
    Why dost thou thus,
Through windows and through curtains call on us?
Must to thy motions lovers' seasons run?
    Saucy pedantic wretch, go chide
    Late school-boys, and sour 'prentices,
  Go tell court-huntsmen that the King will ride,
  Call country ants to harvest offices;
Love, all alike, no season knows, nor clime,
Nor hours, days, months, which are the rags of time.

    Thy beams, so reverend and strong
    Why shouldst thou think?
I could eclipse and cloud them with a wink,
But that I would not lose her sight so long:
    If her eyes have not blinded thine,
    Look, and tomorrow late tell me,
  Whether both the Indias of spice and mine
  Be where thou left'st them, or lie here with me.
Ask for those kings whom thou saw'st yesterday,
And thou shalt hear, "All here in one bed lay."

She's all States, and all Princes I;
　　Nothing else is.
Princes do but play us; compared to this,
All honour's mimic; all wealth alchemy.
　　Thou, Sun, art half as happy as we,
　　In that the world's contracted thus;
　　Thine age asks ease, and since thy duties be
　　To warm the world, that's done in warming us.
Shine here to us, and thou art everywhere;
This bed thy centre is, these walls thy sphere.

JOHN DONNE
(1573-1631)

Cynthia, Because Your Horns Look Diverse Ways

CYNTHIA, because your horns look diverse ways,
Now darkened to the East, now to the West;
Then at full glory once in thirty days,
Sense doth believe that change is nature's rest.

Poor earth, that dare presume to judge the sky;
Cynthia is ever round, and never varies;
Shadows and distance do abuse the eye,
And in abused sense, truth oft miscarries:
　　Yet who this language to the People speaks,
　　Opinion's empire, sense's idol breaks.

FULKE GREVILLE, LORD BROOKE
(1554-1628)

Out in the Dark

OUT in the dark over the snow
The fallow fawns invisible go
With the fallow doe;
And the winds blow
Fast as the stars are slow.

Stealthily the dark haunts round
And, when the lamp goes, without sound
At a swifter bound
Than the swiftest hound,
Arrives, and all else is drowned;

And the star and I and wind and deer,
Are in the dark together,—near,
Yet far,—and fear
Drums on my ear
In that sage company drear.

How weak and little is the light,
All the universe of sight,
Love and delight,
Before the might,
If you love it not, of night.

EDWARD THOMAS
(1878-1917)

Field-Glasses

THOUGH buds still speak in hints
And frozen ground has set the flints
As fast as precious stones
And birds perch on the boughs, silent as cones,

Suddenly waked from sloth
Young trees put on a ten years' growth
And stones double their size,
Drawn nearer through field-glasses' greater eyes.

Why I borrow their sight
Is not to give small birds a fright
Creeping up close by inches;
I make the trees come, bringing tits and finches.

I lift a field itself
As lightly as I might a shelf,
And the rooks do not rage
Caught for a moment in my crystal cage.

And while I stand and look,
Their private lives an open book,
I feel so privileged
My shoulders prick, as though they were half-fledged.

ANDREW YOUNG
(1885-1971)

The Matter at the Atom's Core

(85)

THE matter at the atom's core
is energy, in restless store —
    through star-dust interchanging.
A black hole gapes; all life is o'er —
but Doomsday brings a full encore:
the universe explodes once more,
    its debris rearranging.

(86)

The cosmos must be vaster, far,
    than human minds discern;
suppose it has a master—are
    Earth-men his pet concern?

(87)

One species, we, of millions
   on one small satellite
of one small star of billions
   in one galactic light!
What arrogance, to think that he
   might be especially fond
of us, in all this galaxy —
   and galaxies beyond.

(26)

A wanton waste of life prevails,
   and Natural Selection
necessarily entails
   the merciless rejection
of "creatures great and small": there's first
   gross over-propagation,
then the culling—some through thirst;
   some, sickness; some, starvation;
   and others through predation.

(7)

You ask: if not from godhead, whence
Could human values—moral sense —
   conceivably derive?
Co-operation for defence
Evolved through its advantage; hence
   we're social—and survive.

From *Good God!*
BARBARA SMOKER
(1923-   )

Rock Pool

THROUGH film of glass I stare down at an undiscovered
                                        planet:
jewel star ringed with silver, set in jet rock shade—
the stone shore glitters with a galaxy of pools.

Below me, just a finger-touch away,
this new world spreads in miniature:
highways in veins of sands and fine-grained shingle;
metropolis of pebbles;
dark gleaming domes of sea anemone;
minarets, pagodas built of shell;
marquees of delicately fluted limpet.
Encircling this a filigree of forest.
Layer on layer of many coloured branch-fronds
                                        interweave,
cascade in lemon tendrils,
emerald, sherry-brown.

The rock face rainbows down a wealth of strata:
white turns to barnacle-carved beige;
pink, slate, russet merge in umber;
all watered over, dimmed by palest wash of jade.

Tiny boulders rising from the pool bed grow to
                        mountain ranges.
Pores yawn into caverns.
Dents become crevasses.
Cracks, fissures stretch, expand into deep canyons —
huge gorges through the Himalayas.

There are no people here;
only the fragile sculpture of small crabs;
cellophane flick of shrimps that vanish as you see them.
There is no excrement or garbage;
no silted rivers, strontium or diesel fumes.

PAT ARROWSMITH
(1930-   )

Greenhouse

LINE upon line of cuttings,
tangle of tendrils and foliage vibrant
with sap, lit here and there by
geranium flame.

Clusters of fern absorbing the
soils wetness,
breathing out an earthy musk into
the warmed air.

Flower pots crowded into
glowing ranks stretch
away down the staging seemingly
for ever.

The greenhouse pulsates with life.
Populated with plants it is
the world in a bubble —
all we need.

We do not strain to
look beyond the transparent walls
nor remember that glass
is brittle.

We do not notice the
sky outside start to thicken,
turn to steel, descend as though
to crush us.

Are caught unawares by
the thunder's sharp explosion shivering
the fragile structure that
surrounds us.

A hail of silver bullets
strikes the pane above us.
We look up at last
and realise

how thinly screened we are;
how soon our shelter may be shattered,
our world splintered into
smithereens.

PAT ARROWSMITH

PART V
FANTASY

HUMANISTS are human too, and enjoy fantasy as much as anyone else. Fantasy is a means of transcending fear, boredom and sorrow. It is also joie de vivre, ebullience, verbal facility, fun and nonsense. Why choose one poem rather than another? Perhaps memorability is the criterion. "Cottleston Pie" I find unforgettable.

Many religious writings are, I think, fantasy. They are often deeply felt, giving support and solace, and they touch the deepest springs of action. At the same time they may be used by a priesthood, consciously or not, to gain and hold power over others. By using magical words and claiming invention to be true, ambitious men can destroy the reasoning ability of their flock and reduce women to mute subservience. We are all swayed by rhetorical tricks, by atmosphere and by the pressure to conform. It is important to keep cool enough to be aware of the slender line dividing fact from fiction.

It may surprise both Humanists and Christians to see two hymns included. Both, to my mind, are fantasy. "Songs of Thankfulness and Praise" gives some of the Christian message but not persuasively, so that it now seems dated and incredible; "Hark! the Herald-Angels sing", by a much better author and set to Mendelssohn's music, is a beautiful fantasy about birth, and I will be happy to go on singing it every Christmas.

Here in this realm of acknowledged Fantasy we are all entitled to let go, so please enjoy this section without delving too deeply into the Why and Wherefore.

Hello My Fancy

IN melancholic fancy,
Out of myself,
In the vulcan dancy,
All the world surveying,
Nowhere staying,
Just like a fairy elf;
Out o'er the tops of highest mountains skipping,
Out o'er the hill, the trees and valleys tripping,
Out o'er the ocean seas, without an oar or shipping, —
Hallo my fancy, whither wilt thou go?

Amidst the misty vapours
Fain would I know
What doth cause the tapers;
Why the clouds benight us
And affright us,
While we travel here below;
Fain would I know what makes the roaring thunder,
And what these lightnings be that rend the clouds
asunder,
And what these comets are on which we gaze and
wonder —
Hallo my fancy, whither wilt thou go?

Fain would I know the reason
Why the little ant,
All the summer season,
Layeth up provision
On condition
To know no winter's want.
And how housewives, that are so good and painful,
Do unto their husbands prove so good and gainful;
And why the lazy drones to them do prove disdainful—
Hallo my fancy, whither wilt thou go?

Amidst the foamy ocean,
Fain would I know
What doth cause the motion,
And returning
In its journeying,
And doth so seldom swerve?
And how the little fishes that swim beneath salt waters,
Do never blind their eye; methinks it is a matter
An inch above the reach of old Erra Pater! —
Hallo my fancy, whither wilt thou go?

Fain would I be resolved
How things are done;
And where the bull was calved
Of bloody Phalaris,
And where the tailor is
That works to the man 'i the moon!
Fain would I know how Cupid aims so rightly;
And how the little fairies do dance and leap so lightly,
And where fair Cynthia makes her ambles nightly —
Hallo my fancy, whither wilt thou go?

In conceit like Phaeton
I'll mount Phoebus' chair
Having ne'er a hat on,
All my hair a-burning
In my journeying;
Hurrying through the air.
Fain would I hear his fiery horses neighing
And see how they on foamy bits are playing,
All the stars and planets I will be surveying! —
Hallo my fancy, whither wilt thou go?

O from what ground of nature
Dott the pelican,
   That self-devouring creature
   Prove so froward
   And untoward,
Her vitals for to restrain!
And why the subtle fox, while in death's wounds
     a-lying,
Do not lament his pangs by howling and by crying,
And why the milk-swan doth sing while she's a-dying—
   Hallo my fancy, whither wilt thou go?

   Fain would I conclude this,
   At least make essay;
   What similitude is:
   Why fowls of a feather
   Flock and fly together,
   And lambs know beasts of prey;
How Nature's alchemists, these small laborious
     creatures,
Acknowledge still a prince in ordering their matters,
And suffer none to live who slothing lose their
     features—
   Hallo my fancy, whither wilt thou go?

   To know this world's centre
   Height, depth, breadth and length,
   Fain would I adventure
   To search the hid attractions
   Of magnetic actions
   And adamantine strength.
Fain would I know, if in some lofty mountain,
Where the moon sojourns, if there be tree or fountain;
If there be beasts of prey, or yet be fields to hunt in—
   Hallo my fancy, whither wilt thou go?

Hallo my fancy, hallo,
Stay, stay at home with me,
I can no longer follow,
For thou hast betrayed me,
And bewrayed me;
It is too much for thee.
Stay, stay at home with me, leave off thy lofty soaring;
Stay then at home with me, and on thy books be
        poring;
For he that goes abroad, lays little up in storing —
Thou'rt welcome my fancy, welcome home to me.

WILLIAM CLELAND
(1661?-1689)

On First Looking into Chapman's Homer

MUCH have I travell'd in the realms of gold,
    And many goodly states and kingdoms seen;
    Round many western islands have I been
Which bards in fealty to Apollo hold.
Oft of one wide expanse had I been told
    That deep-brow'd Homer ruled as his demesne;
    Yet did I never breathe its pure serene
Till I heard Chapman speak out loud and bold:
Then felt I like some watcher of the skies
    When a new planet swims into his ken;
Or like stout Cortez when with eagle eyes
    He star'd at the Pacific—and all his men
Look'd at each other with a wild surmise —
    Silent, upon a peak in Darien.

JOHN KEATS
(1795-1821)

A Song for St Cecilia's Day, 1687

FROM harmony, from heavenly harmony
    This universal frame began:
When nature underneath a heap
    Of jarring atoms lay,
  And could not heave her head,
The tuneful voice was heard from high,
    "Arise ye more than dead!"
Then cold, and hot, and moist, and dry,
   In order to their stations leap,
    And Music's power obey.
From harmony, from heavenly harmony
    This universal frame began:
    From harmony to harmony
Through all the compass of the notes it ran,
The diapason closing full in Man.

What passion cannot Music raise and quell?
    When Jubal struck the chorded shell,
His listening brethren stood around,
    And, wondering, on their faces fell
To worship that celestial sound:
Less than a God they thought there could not dwell
    Within the hollow of that shell,
    That spoke so sweetly, and so well.
What passion cannot Music raise and quell?

    The trumpet's loud clangour
      Excites us to arms,
    With shrill notes of anger,
      And mortal alarms.

    The double double double beat
      Of the thundering drum
      Cries Hark! the foes come;
    Charge, charge, 'tis too late to retreat!

    The soft complaining flute,
    In dying notes, discovers
    The woes of hopeless lovers,
Whose dirge is whisper'd by the warbling lute.

Sharp violins proclaim
Their jealous pangs and desperation,
Fury, frantic indignation,
Depth of pains, and height of passion,
  For the fair, disdainful dame.

  But O, what art can teach,
  What human voice can reach
    The sacred organ's praise?
  Notes inspiring holy love,
Notes that wing their heavenly ways
  To mend the choirs above.

Orpheus could lead the savage race;
And trees unrooted left their place,
  Sequacious of the lyre;
But bright Cecilia rais'd the wonder higher:
When to her organ vocal breath was given,
  An angel heard, and straight appear'd
  Mistaking Earth for Heaven.

Grand Chorus
As from the power of sacred lays
  The spheres began to move,
And sung the great Creator's praise
  To all the Blest above;
So when the last and dreadful hour
This crumbling pageant shall devour,
The trumpet shall be heard on high,
The dead shall live, the living die,
And Music shall untune the sky.

JOHN DRYDEN
(1631-1700)

Orpheus

ORPHEUS with his lute made trees
And the mountain tops that freeze
   Bow themselves when he did sing:
To his music plants and flowers
Ever sprung; as sun and showers
   There had made a lasting spring.

Every thing that heard him play,
Even the billows of the sea,
   Hung their heads and then lay by.
In sweet music is such art,
   Killing care and grief of heart
   Fall asleep, or, hearing, die.

WILLIAM SHAKESPEARE
(1564-1616)

To the Muses

WHETHER on Ida's shady brow,
   Or in the chambers of the East,
The chambers of the Sun, that now
   From ancient melody have ceased;

Whether in Heaven ye wander fair,
   Or the green corners of the earth,
Or the blue regions of the air
   Where the melodious winds have birth;

Whether on crystal rocks ye rove,
   Beneath the bosom of the sea,
Wandering in many a coral grove;
   Fair Nine, forsaking Poetry;

How have you left the ancient love
   That bards of old enjoy'd in you!
The languid strings do scarcely move,
   The sound is forced, the notes are few.

WILLIAM BLAKE
(1757-1827)

Letter to Christine de Pisan (1365-1431) during a Pause in Translating Her into English

CHRISTINE, Christine!
What did you mean?
What is this word
I've never heard
Before? And why
Oh why can't I
Find it, tiny
Shard of shiny
Verb in the book
Where I look?
Middle French
On the turn,
What a wrench
To try to learn
Your French, Christine!
Oh, what *did* you mean?
Wish I knew
Whether you
Had meant to say
It's just this way;
Wish that you
Could send a few
Words to me
Just to see,
Smuggled out
Of the stout redoubt
Of the Count of Time
To say that I'm
Doing O.K.
What do you say?

SARAH LAWSON
(1943-   )

Sally Brown

Young Ben he was a nice young man,
  A carpenter by trade;
And he fell in love with Sally Brown,
  That was a lady's maid.

But as they fetch'd a walk one day,
  They met a press-gang crew;
And Sally she did faint away,
  Whilst Ben he was brought to.

The Boatswain swore with wicked words,
  Enough to shock a saint,
But though she did seem in a fit,
  'Twas nothing but a feint.

"Come, girl," said he, "hold up your head,
  He'll be as good as me;
For when your swain is in our boat,
  A boatswain he will be."

So when they'd made their game of her
  And taken off her elf,
She roused, and found she only was
  A-coming to herself.

"And is he gone, and is he gone?"
  She cried and wept outright:
"Then will I to the water side
  And see him out of sight."

A waterman came up to her,
  "Now, young woman," said he,
"If you weep on so, you will make
  Eye-water in the sea."

"Alas! they've taken my beau, Ben,
  To sail with old Benbow;"
And her woe began to run afresh,
  As if she'd said, Gee woe!

Says he, "They've only taken him
    To the Tender-ship, you see;"
"The Tender-ship," cried Sally Brown,
    "What a hard-ship that must be!

"O! would I were a mermaid now,
    For then I'd follow him;
But, oh!—I'm not a fish-woman,
    And so I cannot swim.

"Alas! I was not born beneath
    'The Virgin and the scales',
So I must curse my cruel stars,
    And walk about in Wales."

Now Ben had sail'd to many a place
    That's underneath the world;
But in two years the ship came home,
    And all the sails were furl'd.

But when he call'd on Sally Brown,
    To see how she got on,
He found she'd got another Ben,
    Whose Christian-name was John.

"O Sally Brown, O Sally Brown,
    How could you serve me so,
I've met with many a breeze before,
    But ne'er such a blow!"

Then reading on his 'bacco box
    He heav'd a heavy sigh,
And then began to eye his pipe,
    And then to pipe his eye.

And then he tried to sing "All's Well,"
    But could not, though he tried;
His head was turn'd, and so he chew'd
    His pigtail till he died.

His death, which happen'd in his berth
  At forty-odd befell:
They went and told the sexton, and
  The sexton toll'd the bell.

THOMAS HOOD
(1799-1845)

How Many Miles to Babylon

HOW many miles to Babylon?
Three score miles and ten.
Can I get there by candlelight?
Yes, and back again.
If your heels are nimble and tight,
You may get there by candlelight.

ANON
(1805)

Westminster Drollery

I SAW a peacock with a fiery tail
I saw a blazing comet drop down hail
I saw a cloud with ivy circled round
I saw a sturdy oak creep on the ground
I saw a pismire swallow up a whale
I saw a raging sea brim full of ale
I saw a Venice glass sixteen foot deep
I saw a well full of men's tears that weep
I saw their eyes all in a flame of fire
I saw a house as big as the moon and higher
I saw the sun even in the midst of night
I saw a Man who saw this wondrous sight.

ANON
(1671)

I Saw a Fish Pond All on Fire

I SAW a fish pond all on fire
I saw a house bow to a squire
I saw a parson twelve feet high
I saw a cottage in the sky
I saw a balloon made of lead
I saw a coffin drop down dead
I saw two sparrows run a race
I saw two horses making lace
I saw a girl just like a cat
I saw a kitten wear a hat
I saw a man who saw these too
And said though strange they all were true.

TRADITIONAL
(Collected 1889)

Cottleston Pie!

COTTLESTON, Cottleston, Cottleston Pie!
A fly can't bird, but a bird can fly —
A fish can't whistle and neither can I —
Why does a chicken, I don't know why!
Ask me a riddle, and I reply:
Cottleston, Cottleston, Cottleston Pie!

A. A. MILNE
(1882-1956)

There Was an Old Man . . .

THERE was an Old Man of Thermopylae,
Who never did anything properly;
But they said: "If you choose
To boil Eggs in your Shoes,
You shall never remain in Thermopylae."

There was an Old Man of Coblenz,
The length of whose legs was immense;
He went with one prance
From Turkey to France,
That surprising Old Man Of Coblenz.

EDWARD LEAR
(1812-1888)

167

The Mad Gardener's Song

HE thought he saw an Elephant,
  That practised on a fife:
He looked again, and found it was
  A letter from his wife.
"At length I realize," he said,
  "The bitterness of Life!"

He thought he saw a Buffalo
  Upon the chimney-piece:
He looked again, and found it was
  His Sister's Husband's Niece.
"Unless you leave this house," he said,
  "I'll send for the Police!"

He thought he saw a Rattlesnake
  That questioned him in Greek:
He looked again, and found it was
  The Middle of Next Week.
"The one thing I regret," he said,
  "Is that it cannot speak!"

He thought he saw a Banker's Clerk
  Descending from the bus:
He looked again, and found it was
  A Hippopotamus:
"If this should stay to dine," he said,
  "There won't be much for us!"

He thought he saw a Kangaroo
  That worked a coffee-mill:
He looked again, and found it was
  A Vegetable-Pill.
"Were I to swallow this," he said,
  "I should be very ill!"

He thought he saw a Coach-and-Four
  That stood beside his bed:
He looked again, and found it was
  A Bear without a Head.
"Poor thing," he said, "poor silly thing! —
  It's waiting to be fed!"

He thought he saw an Albatross
That fluttered round the lamp:
He looked again, and found it was
A Penny-Postage-Stamp.
"You'd best be getting home," he said:
"The nights are very damp!"

He thought he saw a Garden-Door
That opened with a key:
He looked again, and found it was
A Double Rule of Three:
"And all its mystery," he said,
"Is clear as day to me!"

He thought he saw an Argument
That proved he was the Pope:
He looked again, and found it was
A Bar of Mottled Soap.
"A fact so dread," he faintly said,
"Extinguishes all hope!"

LEWIS CARROLL
(1832-1898)

Three Men of Gotham

SEAMEN three! What men be ye?
Gotham's three wise men we be.
Whither in your bowl so free?
To rake the moon from out the sea.
The bowl goes trim. The moon doth shine.
And our ballast is old wine. —
And your ballast is old wine.

Who art thou, so fast adrift?
I am he they call Old Care.
Here on board we will thee lift.
No: I may not enter there.
Wherefore so? 'Tis Jove's decree,
In a bowl Care may not be. —
In a bowl Care may not be.

Fear ye not the waves that roll?
No: in charmed bowl we swim.
What the charm that floats the bowl?
Water may not pass the brim.
The bowl goes trim. The moon doth shine.
And our ballast is old wine. —
And your ballast is old wine.

THOMAS LOVE PEACOCK
(1785-1866)

The Dancing Cabman

ALONE on the lawn
     The cabman dances;
In the dew of dawn
     He kicks and prances.
His bowler is set
     On his bullet-head.
For his boots are wet,
     And his aunt is dead.
There on the lawn,
     As the light advances,
On the tide of the dawn,
     The cabman dances.

Swift and strong
     As a garden roller,
He dances along
     In his little bowler,
Skimming the lawn
     With royal grace,
The dew of dawn
     On his great red face.
To fairy flutes,
     As the light advances,
In square black boots
     The cabman dances.

BEACHCOMBER (H. B. MORTON)

Country Stuff

As Oi wur a-warkin' in Zquoire Daamson's laane,
  (Wi' a raanty-daanty-diddy)
Oi chaanced vur ter zee moi sweet 'eart agaain
  (Wi' a raanty-diddy-o-do).
'Er wus droivin' coos in mook and durt,
In 'er mother's shoes an' 'er vayther's shurt,
'Er uncle's 'at, an 'er zister's skurt
(Wi' a raanty-rochity-ree).

BEACHCOMBER (H. B. MORTON)

Ancient Music

WINTER is icummen in,
Lhude sing Goddamm,
Raineth drop and staineth slop,
And how the wind doth ramm!
  Sing: Goddamm.
Skiddeth bus and sloppeth us,
An ague hath my ham.
Freezeth river, turneth liver,
  Damn you, sing: Goddamm.
Goddamm, Goddamm, 'tis why I am, Goddamm,
  So 'gainst the winter's balm.
Sing Goddamm, damm, sing Goddam,
Sing Goddamm, sing Goddamm, DAMM.

*Note: this is not folk music, but Dr Ker writes that the tune is
to be found under the Latin words of a very ancient cannon.
(E. P.)*

EZRA POUND
(1885-1972)

The Microbe

THE Microbe is so very small
You cannot make him out at all,
But many sanguine people hope
To see him through a microscope.
His jointed tongue that lies beneath
A hundred curious rows of teeth;
His seven tufted tails with lots
Of lovely pink and purple spots,
On each of which a pattern stands,
Composed of forty separate bands;
His eyebrows of a tender green;
All these have never yet been seen —
But Scientists, who ought to know,
Assure us that they must be so. . . .
Oh! let us never, never doubt
What nobody is sure about!

HILAIRE BELLOC
(1870-1953)

The First Men on Mercury

— WE come in peace from the third planet.
Would you take us to your leader?

— Bawr stretter! Bawr. Stretterhawl?

— This is a little plastic model
Of the solar system, with working parts.
You are here and we are there and we
are here now with you, is this clear?

— Gawl horrop. Bawr. Abawrhannahanna!

— Where we come from is blue and white
with brown, you see we call the brown
here "land", the blue is "sea", and the white
is "clouds" over land and sea, we live
on the surface of the brown land,
all round is sea and clouds. We are "men".
Men come —

172

—Glawp men! Gawrbenner menko. Menhawl?

— Men come in peace from the third planet
which we call "earth". We are earthmen.
Take us earthmen to your leader.

— Thmen? Thmen? Bawr. Bawrhossop.
Yuleeda tan hanna. Harrabost yuleeda.

— I am the yuleeda. You see my hands,
we carry no benner, we come in peace.
The space ways are all stretterhawl.

— Glawn peacemen all horrobhanna tantko!
Tan come at'mstrossop. Glawp yuleeda!

— Atoms are peacegawl in our harraban.
Menbat worrabost from tan hannahanna.

—ou men we know bawrhossoptant. Bawr.
We know yuleeda. Go strawg backspetter quick.

— We cantantabawr, tantingko backspetter now!

— Banghapper now! Yes, third planet backspetter now!
Yuleeda will go back blue, white, brown
nowhanna! There is no more talk.

— Gawl han fasthapper?

— No. You must go back to your planet.
Go back in peace, take what you have gained
but quickly.

— Stretterworra gawl, gawl. . . .

— Of course, but nothing is ever the same,
now is it? You'll remember Mercury.

EDWIN MORGAN
(1920-   )

173

The Scapegoat

BURDENED with great iniquity and pain
In the vast wilderness of human scorn,
The Scapegoat travels on towards the dawn
Another outcast yet, another Cain.
No herdsman claims him now, from him in vain
All pasture-lands and bright sweet streams are torn,
And leaders' bells, and struggles horn to horn
In the green valleys of his old domain.

In some precipitous ravine of stones
He stumbles on his predecessor's bones
Pale sepulchre of unresisted blame;
Then idly, where a few sparse grasses grow
He crops the stunted nettles of his woe,
And drinks the brackish waters of his shame.

YVONNE FFRENCH

The Witch

NOW I'm furnished for the flight,
Now I go, now I fly,
Malkin my sweet spirit and I.
O, what a dainty pleasure 'tis
To ride in the air
When the moon shines fair,
And sing and dance and toy and kiss.
Over woods, high rocks, and mountains,
Over seas, our mistress' fountains,
Over steeples, towers, and turrets,
We fly by night, 'mongst troops of spirits.
No ring of bells to our ears sounds,
No howls of wolves, no yelp of hounds.
No, not the noise of water's breach,
Or cannon's throat our height can reach.

THOMAS MIDDLETON
(1580-1627)

174

The Fairies

UP the airy mountain,
  Down the rushy glen,
We daren't go a-hunting
  For fear of little men;
Wee folk, good folk,
  Trooping all together;
Green jacket, red cap,
  And white owl's feather!

Down along the rocky shore
  Some make their home,
They live on crispy pancakes
  Of yellow tide-foam;
Some in the reeds
  Of the black mountain lake,
With frogs for their watch-dogs
  All night awake.

High on the hill-top
  The old King sits;
He is now so old and grey
  He's nigh lost his wits.
With a bridge of white mist
  Columbkill he crosses,
On his stately journeys
  From Slieveleague to Rosses;
Or going up with music
  On cold starry nights
To sup with the Queen
  Of the gay Northern Lights.

They stole little Bridget
 For seven years long;
When she came down again
 Her friends were all gone.
They took her lightly back,
 Between the night and morrow,
They thought that she was fast asleep,
 But she was dead with sorrow.
They have kept her ever since
 Deep within the lake,
On a bed of flag-leaves,
 Watching till she wake.

By the craggy hill-side,
 Through the mosses bare,
They have planted thorn-trees
 For pleasure here and there.
If any man so daring
 As dig them up in spite,
He shall find their sharpest thorns
 In his bed at night.

Up the airy mountain,
 Down the rushy glen,
We daren't go a-hunting
 For fear of little men;
Wee folk, good folk,
 Trooping all together;
Green jacket, red cap,
 And white owl's feather!

WILLIAM ALLINGHAM
(1824-1889)

Dese Bones Gwine to Rise Again

DE Lord he thought he'd make a man —
Dese bones gwine to rise again;
Made him out-a dirt an' a little bit o' sand —
Dese bones gwine to rise again.

   I know it, 'deed I know it,
   Dese bones gwine to rise again.

Adam was de fust he made —
He put him on de bank an' lay him in de shade —

Thought He'd made a ooman too —
Didn't know 'xactly what to do —

Took a rib from Adam's side —
Made Miss Eve for to be his bride —

Put 'em in a gyarden, rich an' fair —
Tol' 'em dey might eat whatever wuz dere —

But to one tree dey mus' not go —
Mus' leave de apples dere to grow —

Ol' Miss Eve come walkin' roun' —
Spied a tree all loaded down —

Sarpint quoiled around a chunk —
At Miss Eve his eye he wunk —

Firs' she took a little pull —
Den she fill her apron full —

Den Adam took a little slice —
Smack his lips an' say 'twas nice —

De Lord He come a-wanderin' roun' —
Spied dem peelin's on de groun' —

De Lord He speaks wid a monstrus voice —
Shuck dis ol' worl' to its ve'y joists —

"Adam, Adam, where art thou?"
"Heah, Marse Lord, Ise a-comin' now".

"Stole my apples, I believe?"
"No, Marse Lord, but I spec' it wuz Eve".

De Lord He riz up in His wrath —
Told 'em, "Yo' beat it down de path."

"Out o' dis gyarden you mus' git.
"Earn yo' livin' by yo' sweat."

He put an angel at de do'
Tol' 'em not to never come dere no mo' —

Ob dis tale dere ain' no mo' —
Dese bones gwine to rise again.
Eve eat de apple, gib Adam de co' —
Dese bones gwine to rise again.

Refrain:

I know it, 'deed I know it,
Dese bones gwine to rise again.

ANON

The Theology of Bongwi, the Baboon

THIS is the wisdom of the Ape
  Who yelps beneath the Moon —
'Tis God who made me in His shape
  He is a Great Baboon.
'Tis he who tilts the moon askew
  And fans the forest trees,
The heavens which are broad and blue
  Provide him his trapeze;
He swings with tail divinely bent
  Around those azure bars
And munches to his Soul's content
  The kernels of the stars;
And when I die, His loving care
  Will raise me from the sod
To learn the perfect Mischief there,
  The Nimbleness of God.

ROY CAMPBELL
(1902-1957)

Hymn

SONGS of thankfulness and praise,
Jesu, Lord, to Thee we raise,
Manifested by the star
To the sages from afar;
Branch of royal David's stem
In Thy Birth at Bethlehem;
Anthems be to Thee addrest,
God in Man made manifest.

Manifest at Jordan's stream.
Prophet, Priest, and King supreme;
And at Cana wedding-guest
In thy Godhead manifest;
Manifest in power Divine,
Changing water into wine;
Anthems be to Thee addrest,
God in Man made manifest.

Manifest in making whole
Palsied limbs and fainting soul;
Manifest in valiant fight,
Quelling all the devil's might;
Manifest in gracious will,
Ever bringing good from ill;
Anthems be to Thee addrest,
God in Man made manifest.

Sun and Moon shall darken'd be,
Stars shall fall, the heavens shall flee;
Christ will then like lightning shine,
All will see His glorious Sign;
All will then the trumpet hear,
All will see the Judge appear;
Thou by all wilt be confest,
God in Man made manifest.

Grant us grace to see Thee, Lord,
Mirror'd in Thy holy Word;
May we imitate Thee now,
And be pure, as pure art Thou;
That we like to Thee may be
At Thy great Epiphany,
And may praise Thee, ever Blest,
God in Man made manifest.

BISHOP C. WORDSWORTH
(1807-1885)

Hymn

HARK! the herald-Angels sing
Glory to the new-born King;
Peace on earth and mercy mild,
God and sinners reconciled;
Joyful all ye nations rise,
Join the triumph of the skies;
With the Angelic host proclaim,
"Christ is born in Bethlehem."
Hark! the herald-Angels sing
Glory to the new-born King.

Christ, by highest Heav'n adored,
Christ, the Everlasting Lord,
Late in time behold him come,
Offspring of a Virgin's womb!
Veil'd in flesh the Godhead see!
Hail, the Incarnate Deity!
Pleased as Man with man to dwell,
Jesus, our Emmanuel.
Hark! the herald-Angels sing
Glory to the new-born King.

Hail, the heaven-born Prince of Peace!
Hail, the Sun of righteousness!
Light and life to all He brings,
Risen with healing in His wings.
Mild He lays His glory by,
Born that man no more may die,
Born to raise the sons of earth,
Born to give them second birth.
Hark! the herald-Angels sing
Glory to the new-born King.

CHARLES WESLEY
(1707-1788)

The Day Before the Last Day

IF it could come to pass, and all kill all
And in a day or week we could destroy
Ourselves, that is the beginning only
Of the destruction, for so we murder all
That ever has been, all species and forms,
Man and woman and child, beast and bird,
Tree, flower and herb, and that by which they were
    known,
Sight and hearing and touch, feeling and thought,
And memory of our friends among the dead.
If there were only a single ear that listening heard
A footstep coming nearer, it would bring
Annunciation of the world's resurrection.
A sound! We would not know even the silence
Where all was now as if it had never been.

Mechanical parody of the Judgment Day
That does not judge but only deals damnation.
Let us essay a hypothetical picture.

"All these and all alone in death's last day."
Before them stretches the indifferent ocean
Where no wave lifts its head and stagnant water
Lies spent against the shore. Yet as they wait
A wan light from the east falls on their faces
And they cannot bear the light, and hide in the
  ground,
Yet have no comfort there, for all are alone.
And there awaken the dark ancestral dreams.
They dream that the grave and the sea give up their
  dead
In wonder at the news of the death of death,
Hearing that death itself is balked by death.

And those who were drowned a year or a thousand
  years
Come out with staring eyes, foam on their faces,
And quaint sea-creatures fixed like jewelled worms
Upon their salt-white crowns, sea-tangle breasts,
That they, the once dead, might know the second
  death.
And then a stir and rumour break their dream,
As men and women at the point of death
Rise from their beds and clasp the ground in hope
Imploring sanctuary from grass and root
That never failed them yet and seemed immortal.
And women faint with child-birth lay their babes
Beside them on the earth and turn away
And lovers two by two estranged for ever
Lie each in place without a parting look.
And the dying awakened know
That the generous do not try to help their neighbours,
Nor the feeble and greedy ask for succour,
Nor the fastidious complain of their company,
Nor the ambitious dream of a great chance lost
Nor the preacher try to save one soul. For all
Think only of themselves and curse the faithless earth.
The sun rises above the sea, and they look and think:
"We shall not watch its setting." And all get up
And stare at the sun. But they hear no great voice
    crying:
"There shall be no more time, nor death, nor change,
Nor fear, nor hope, nor longing, nor offence,

Nor need, nor shame." But all are silent, thinking:
"Choose! Choose again, you who have chosen this!
Too late! Too late!"
And then: "Where and by whom shall we be
    remembered?"

Imaginary picture of a stationary fear.

EDWIN MUIR
(1887-1959)

PART VI

FACING THE WORLD

THIS final part of the anthology is concerned with how to
live. Earlier parts have considered human life, religion,
time, the world of nature, and the imagination. Now we
have to choose, decide and act. Whatever the extenuating
circumstances may be, we have to be prepared to answer
the question: "Why did you . . ?". We have to justify
ourselves to ourselves, our fellows and posterity. Even if we
decide not to choose, this is also a decision; and if we
follow the guidance of a priest or guru, that is also a
decision for which we are responsible. "Look if you like,
but you will have to leap" as Auden puts it.

Broadly speaking these poems divide first into classical
categories of Hedonist or Stoic counselling: enjoyment or
endurance. Christianity brings in ideas of Love or Duty.
Elizabeth Daryush heralds a forward-looking era.
Existentialism reveals the absurdity of life: we cannot plan
ahead, since we don't know how long we shall live.
Relativity tells us to reverse long-held illusions: "All
absolutes the Enemy". We have to take decisions without
time or data. In short, we have to do the best we can.

Despite all this, the poets' main drive is life-affirming,
often rapturous. A poem represents the transcendence of
a struggle: to express is to overcome. So Pearse in his
"Renunciation" reaffirms an agonised decision to lay
down his rich life for an ideal cause. So Keats overcomes
the torture of his illness by writing of beauty. With the
help of brief satire, Michael Carrie copes with the
hypocrisy of the very rich; and by writing of the sea, St
John Gogarty comes to terms with the squalor of his life.

John Adlard's "Signalman at Treblinka" and Thom
Gunn's "Epitaph for Anton Schmidt" contrast the
unthinking colluder with the courageous resister. These
poems interest me particularly. as I was caught up in the
rise of Hitler's Nazism and often wondered how I would
react to being woken at 3 a.m. by the secret police.

The anthology ends with several highly individual
poems, each dealing with an important area of
responsibility. They raise great contemporary and

perennial issues, moral and political. Muriel Rukeyser asserts that Peace is not a failure of will but a positive thing; D. H. Lawrence's "Money-Madness" is even more relevant now than when he wrote it; Earle Birney states that "We contrived the power that snuffed us. . . . No one bound prometheus Himself chained".

Finally, in the passage which closes both his long poem "Winged Chariot" and this anthology, Walter de la Mare declares that our best inspiration is in the here and now, and that only our own constant, devoted effort can maintain and further what we hold most dear. It is really up to us.

A Thing of Beauty

A THING of beauty is a joy for ever:
Its loveliness increases; it will never
Pass into nothingness; but still will keep
A bower quiet for us, and a sleep
Full of sweet dreams, and health, and quiet breathing.
Therefore, on every morrow, are we wreathing
A flowery band to bind us to the earth,
Spite of despondence, of the inhuman dearth
Of noble natures, of the gloomy days,
Of all the unhealthy and o'er-darkened ways
Made for our searching: yes, in spite of all,
Some shape of beauty moves away the pall
From our dark spirits. Such the sun, the moon,
Trees old and young, sprouting a shady boon
For simple sheep; and such are daffodils
With the green world they live in; and clear rills
That for themselves a cooling covert make
'Gainst the hot season; the mid-forest brake,
Rich with a sprinkling of fair musk-rose blooms:
And such too is the grandeur of the dooms
We have imagined for the mighty dead;
All lovely tales that we have heard or read:
An endless fountain of immortal drink,
Pouring unto us from the heaven's brink.

Nor do we merely feel these essences
For one short hour; no, even as the trees
That whisper round a temple become soon
Dear as the temple's self, so does the moon,
The passion poesy, glories infinite,
Haunt us till they become a cheering light
Unto our souls, and bound to us so fast,
That, whether there be shine, or gloom o'ercast,
They alway must be with us, or we die.

From *Endymion, Book I*
JOHN KEATS
(1795-1821)

It is Not Growing like a Tree

IT is not growing like a tree
In bulk, doth make men better be;
Or standing long an oak, three hundred year,
To fall a log at last, dry, bald, and sere:
    A lily of a day
    Is fairer far in May,
Although it fall and die that night;
It was the plant and flower of light.
    In small proportions we just beauties see;
    And in short measures, life may perfect be.

From *A Part of an Ode*
BEN JONSON
(1573-1637)

My Heart Leaps Up

MY heart leaps up when I behold
A rainbow in the sky:
So was it when my life began:
So is it now I am a man:
So be it when I shall grow old,
Or let me die!
The Child is father of the Man;
And I could wish my days to be
Bound each to each by natural piety.

WILLIAM WORDSWORTH
(1770-1850)

Sonnet CXVI

LET me not to the marriage of true minds
Admit impediments. Love is not love
Which alters when it alteration finds,
Or bends with the remover to remove.
O, no! It is an ever-fixed mark,
That looks on tempests and is never shaken;
It is the star to every wandering bark,
Whose worth's unknown, although his height be taken.
Love's not Time's fool, though rosy lips and cheeks
Within his bending sickle's compass come;
Love alters not with his brief hours and weeks,
But bears it out even to the edge of doom.
If this be error, and upon me proved,
I never writ, nor no man ever loved.

WILLIAM SHAKESPEARE
(1564-1616)

Be Free

BE free, all worthy spirits,
And stretch yourselves, for greatness and for height:
Untruss your slaveries: you have height enough
Beneath this steep heaven to use all your reaches.
Give me a spirit that on this life's rough sea
Loves t'have his sails fill'd with a lusty wind,
Even till his sail-yards tremble, his masts crack,
And his rapt ship run on her side so low
That she drinks water and her keel plows air.

From *Byron's Conspiracy*
GEORGE CHAPMAN
(c1559-1634)

Sweet Content

ART thou poor, yet hast thou golden slumbers?
O sweet content!
Art thou rich, yet is thy mind perplex'd?
O punishment!
Dost thou laugh to see how fools are vex'd
To add to golden numbers golden numbers?
O sweet content! O sweet, O sweet content!
Work apace, apace, apace, apace;
Honest labour bears a lovely face;
Then hey nonny nonny—hey nonny nonny!

Canst drink the waters of the crisped spring?
O sweet content!
Swim'st thou in wealth, yet sinks't in thine own tears?
O punishment!
Then he that patiently want's burden bears,
No burden bears, but is a king, a king!
O sweet content, O sweet, O sweet content!
Work apace, apace, apace, apace;
Honest labour bears a lovely face;
Then hey nonny nonny—hey nonny nonny!

THOMAS DEKKER
(c1570-1632)

The Choir Invisible

O MAY I join the choir invisible
Of those immortal dead who live again
In minds made better by their presence: live
In pulses stirred to generosity,
In deeds of daring rectitude, in scorn
For miserable aims that end with self,
In thought sublime that pierce the night like stars,
And with their mild persistence urge man's search
To vaster issues.
So to live is heaven:
To make undying music in the world,
Breathing as beauteous order that controls
With growing sway the growing life of man.

So we inherit that sweet purity
For which we struggled, failed, and agonized
With widening retrospect that bred despair.
Rebellious flesh that would not be subdued,
A vicious parent shaming still its child
Poor anxious penitence, is quick dissolved;
Its discords, quenched by meeting harmonies,
Die in the large and charitable air.
And all our rarer, better, truer self,
That sobb'd religiously in yearning song,
That watch'd to ease the burthen of the world,
Laboriously tracing what must be,
And what may yet be better—saw within
A worthier image for the sanctuary,
And shaped it forth before the multitude
Divinely human, raising worship so
To higher reverence more mix'd with love —
That better self shall live till human Time
Shall fold its eyelids, and the human sky
Be gather'd like a scroll within the tomb
Unread for ever.
       This is life to come,
Which martyr'd men have made more glorious
For us who strive to follow. May I reach
That purest heaven, be to other souls
The cup of strength in some great agony,
Enkindle generous ardour, feed pure love,
Beget the smiles that have no cruelty —
Be the sweet presence of a good diffused,
And in diffusion ever more intense.
So shall I join the choir invisible
Whose music is the gladness of the world.

GEORGE ELIOT
(MARY ANN EVANS)
(1819-1880)

Sonnet: Political Greatness

NOR happiness, nor majesty, nor fame,
Nor peace, nor strength, nor skill in arms or arts,
Shepherd those herds whom tyranny makes tame;
Verse echoes not one beating of their hearts,
History is but the shadow of their shame,
Art veils her glass, or from the pageant starts
As to oblivion their blind millions fleet,
Staining that Heaven with obscene imagery
Of their own likeness. What are numbers knit
By force or custom? Man who man would be,
Must rule the empire of himself; in it
Must be supreme, establishing his throne
On vanquished will, quelling the anarchy
Of hopes and fears, being himself alone.

PERCY BYSSHE SHELLEY
(1792-1822)

The One Mystery

'TIS idle! we exhaust and squander
    The glittering mine of thought in vain;
All-baffled reason cannot wander
    Beyond her chain.
The flood of life runs dark—dark clouds
    Make lampless night around its shore:
The dead, where are they? In their shrouds —
    Man knows no more.

Evoke the ancient and the past,
    Will one illumining star arise?
Or must the film, from first to last,
    O'erspread thine eyes?
When life, love, glory, beauty, wither,
    Will wisdom's page, or science's chart,
Map out for thee the region whither
    Their shades depart?

Supposest thou the wondrous powers,
　To high imagination given,
Pale types of what shall yet be ours,
　When earth is heaven?
When this decaying shell is cold,
　Oh! sayest thou the soul shall climb
That magic mount she trod of old,
　Ere childhood's time?

And shall the sacred pulse that thrilled
　Thrill once again to glory's name?
And shall the conquering love that filled
　All earth with flame,
Reborn, revived, renewed, immortal,
　Resume his reign in prouder might,
A sun beyond the ebon portal
　Of death and night?

No more, no more,—with aching brow
　And restless heart, and burning brain,
We ask the When, the Where, the How,
　And ask in vain.
And all philosophy, all faith,
　All earthly,—all celestial lore,
Have but one voice, which only saith —
　Endure, adore!

JAMES CLARENCE MANGAN
(1803-1849)

The World's a Bubble

THE world's a bubble, and the life of man
　Less than a span,
In his conception wretched, from the womb,
　So to the tomb;
Curst from the cradle, and brought up to years,
　With cares and fears.
Who then to frail mortality shall trust,
But limns on water, or but writes in dust.

Yet since with sorrow here we live oppressed,
   What life is best?
Courts are but only superficial schools
   To dandle fools.
The rural parts are turned into a den
   Of savage men.
And where's a city from all vice so free,
   But may be termed the worst of all the three?

Domestic cares afflict the husband's bed,
   Or pains his head.
Those that live single take it for a curse,
   Or do things worse.
Some would have children; those that have them none,
   Or wish them gone.
What is it then to have or have no wife,
   But single thraldom, or a double strife?

Our own affections still at home to please
   Is a disease;
To cross the sea to any foreign soil,
   Perils and toil.
Wars with their noise affright us; when they cease,
   W'are worse in peace.
What then remains, but that we still should cry,
   Not to be born, or being born to die?

FRANCIS BACON
(1561-1626)

Is it so small a thing

Is it so small a thing
To have enjoy'd the sun,
To have lived light in the spring,
To have loved, to have thought, to have done;
To have advanced true friends, and beat down baffling
   foes;

That we must feign a bliss
Of doubtful future date,
And whilst we dream on this
Lose all our present state,
And relegate to worlds yet distant our repose?

Not much, I know, you prize
What pleasure may be had,
Who look on life with eyes
Estranged, like mine, and sad:
And yet the village churl feels the truth more than you;

Who's loth to leave this life
Which to him little yields:
His hard-task'd sunburnt wife,
His often-labour'd fields;
The boors with whom he talk'd, the country spots he
    knew.

But thou, because thou hear'st
Men scoff at Heaven and Fate;
Because the gods thou fear'st
Fail to make blest thy state,
Tremblest, and wilt not dare to trust the joys there are.

I say, Fear not! life still
Leaves human effort scope.
But, since life teems with ill,
Nurse no extravagant hope.
Because thou must not dream, thou need'st not then
    despair.

From *Empedocles on Etna*
MATTHEW ARNOLD
(1822-1888)

And If I Did, What Then?

"AND if I did, what then?
Are you aggrieved therefore?
The sea hath fish for every man,
And what would you have more?"

Thus did my mistress once
Amaze my mind with doubt;
And popped a question for the nonce
To beat my brains about.

Whereto I thus replied:
"Each fisherman can wish
That all the seas at every tide
Were his alone to fish;

And so did I, in vain;
But since it may not be,
Let such fish there as find the gain,
And leave the loss for me.

And with such luck and loss
I will content myself,
Till tides of turning time may toss
Such fishers on the shelf.

And when they stick on sands,
That every man may see,
Then will I laugh and clap my hands,
As they do now at me."

GEORGE GASCOIGNE
(1542-1577)

Recitative and Air from Dido and Aeneas
(Music by Henry Purcell)

Recitative:
THY hand, Belinda, darkness shades me:
   On thy bosom let me rest:
More I would, but Death invades me:
   Death is now a welcome guest.

194

Air:
When I am laid, am laid in earth,
May my wrongs create
No trouble, no trouble in thy breast;
Remember me, remember me,
But ah! forget my fate.
Remember me, but ah! forget my fate.

NAHUM TATE
(1652-1715)

Weep not Today

WEEP not today: why should this sadness be?
   Learn in present fears
   To o'ermaster those tears
   That unhindered conquer thee.

Think on thy past valour, thy future praise:
   Up, sad heart, nor faint
   In ungracious complaint,
   Or a prayer for better days.

Daily thy life shortens, the grave's dark peace
   Draweth surely nigh,
   When good-night is good-bye;
   For the sleeping shall not cease.

Fight, to be found fighting: nor far away
   Deem, nor strange thy doom.
   Like this sorrow 'twill come,
   And the day will be today.

ROBERT BRIDGES
(1844-1930)

Renunciation

NAKED I saw thee,
O beauty of beauty,
And I blinded my eyes
For fear I should fail.

I heard thy music,
O melody of melody,
And I closed my ears
For fear I should falter.

I tasted thy mouth,
O sweetness of sweetness,
And I hardened my heart
For fear of my slaying.

I blinded my eyes,
And I closed my ears,
I hardened my heart
And I smothered my desire.

I turned my back
On the vision I had shaped,
And to this road before me
I turned my face.

I have turned my face
To this road before me,
To the deed that I see
And the death I shall die.

PATRICK PEARSE
(1879-1916)

The Deserter's Meditation

IF sadly thinking, with spirits sinking,
  Could more than drinking my cares compose,
A cure for sorrow from sighs I'd borrow,
  And hope tomorrow would end my woes.
But as in wailing there's nought availing,
  And Death unfailing will strike the blow,
Then for that reason, and for a season,
  Let us be merry before we go.

To joy a stranger, a way-worn ranger,
  In every danger my course I've run;
Now hope all ending, and death befriending
  His last aid lending, my cares are done.
No more a rover, or hapless lover,
  My griefs are over—my glass runs low;
Then for that reason, and for a season,
  Let us be merry before we go.

JOHN PHILPOT CURRAN
(1750-1817)

Hey Nonny No!

HEY nonny no!
Men are fools that wish to die!
Is't not fine to dance and sing
When the bells of death do ring?
Is't not fine to swim in wine,
And turn upon the toe,
And sing hey nonny no!
When the winds blow and the seas flow?
Hey nonny no!

ANON
(Sixteenth century)

My Sweetest Lesbia

MY sweetest Lesbia, let us live and love;
And though the sager sort our deeds reprove,
Let us not weigh them, heaven's great lamps do dive
Into their west, and straight again revive.
But soon as once set is our little light,
Then must we sleep one ever-during night.

If all would lead their lives in love like me,
Then bloody swords and armour should not be.
No drum nor trumpet peaceful sleeps should move,
Unless alarm came from the camp of Love.
But fools do live and waste their little light,
And seek with pain their ever-during night.

When timely death my life and fortune ends,
Let not my hearse be vext with mourning friends.
But let all lovers rich in triumph come,
And with sweet pastimes grace my happy tomb.
And Lesbia, close up thou my little light,
And crown with love my ever-during night.

THOMAS CAMPION
(1567-1620)

The Passionate Shepherd to His Love

COME live with me, and be my love,
And we will all the pleasures prove
That valleys, groves, hills and fields,
Woods, or steepy mountain yields.

And we will sit upon the rocks,
Seeing the shepherds feed their flocks
By shallow rivers, to whose falls
Melodious birds sing madrigals.

And I will make thee beds of roses,
And a thousand fragrant posies,
A cap of flowers, and a kirtle,
Embroidered all with leaves of myrtle.

A gown made of the finest wool
Which from our pretty lambs we pull,
Fair lined slippers for the cold,
With buckles of the purest gold.

A belt of straw and ivy-buds,
With coral clasps and amber studs,
And if these pleasures may thee move,
Then live with me, and be my love.

The shepherd swains shall dance and sing
For thy delight each May morning.
If these delights thy mind may move,
Come live with me and be my love.

CHRISTOPHER MARLOWE
(1564-1593)

The Nymph's Reply

IF all the world and love were young,
And truth in every shepherd's tongue,
These pretty pleasures might me move
To live with thee and be thy love.

But Time drives flocks from field to fold,
When rivers rage and rocks grow cold,
And Philomel becometh dumb;
The rest complains of cares to come.

The flowers do fade, and wanton fields
To wayward winter reckoning yields;
A honey tongue, a heart of gall
Is fancy's spring, but sorrow's fall.

Thy gowns, thy shoes, thy beds of roses,
Thy cap, thy kirtle, and thy posies,
Soon break, soon wither, soon forgotten,
In folly ripe, in reason rotten.

Thy belt of straw and ivy buds,
Thy coral clasps and amber studs,
All these in me no means can move
To come to thee and be thy love.

But could youth last and love still breed,
Had joys no date, nor age no need,
Then these delights my mind might move
To live with thee and be thy love.

WALTER RALEGH
(1552-1618)

Ringsend
(After reading Tolstoy)

I WILL live in Ringsend
With a red-headed whore,
And the fan-light gone in
Where it lights the hall-door;
And listen each night
For her querulous shout,
As at last she streels in
And the pubs empty out.
To soothe that wild breast
With my old-fangled songs,
Till she feels it redressed
From inordinate wrongs,
Imagined, outrageous,
Preposterous wrongs,
Till peace at last comes,
Shall be all I will do,
Where the little lamp blooms
Like a rose in the stew;
And up the back-garden
The sound comes to me
Of the lapsing, unsoilable,
Whispering sea.

OLIVER ST JOHN GOGARTY
(1878-1957)

Moving In

I WISH you for your birthday as you are,
Inherently happy,
The little girl always shining out of your face
And the woman standing her ground.

Wish you the seldom oceanic earthquake
Which shatters your gaze
Against some previous interior past
And rights you.

Wish you your honesty normal as a tree
Confounding the caws of intellectuals.
When I zip your dress I kiss you on the neck,
A talisman in honour of your pride.

When I hold your head in my hands
It is as of the roundness of Columbus
Thinking the world, "my hands capable of
Designing the earthly sphere."

Your fingers on the piano keys
Or the typewriter keys or on my face
Write identical transcriptions.
Nothing you do is lost in translation.

I am delighted that you loathe Christmas.
I feel the same about Communism.
Let us live in the best possible house,
Selfish and true.

May the Verdi Requiem continue to knock you out
As it does me; fashionable protest art
Continue to infuriate your heart
And make you spill your drink.

Now ideology has had its day
Nothing is more important than your birthday.
Let us have a solid roof over our head
And bless one another.

KARL SHAPIRO
(1913-   )

The Rape of the Lock

Canto V

OH! if to dance all Night, and dress all Day,
Charm'd the Small-pox, or chas'd old Age away;
Who would not scorn what Huswife's Cares produce,
Or who would learn one earthly Thing of Use?
To patch, nay ogle, might become a Saint,
Nor could it sure be such a Sin to paint.
But since, alas! frail Beauty must decay,
Curl'd or uncurl'd, since Locks will turn to grey,
Since painted, or not painted, all shall fade,
And she who scorns a Man, must die a Maid;
What then remains, but well our Pow'r to use,
And keep good Humour still whate'er we lose?
And trust me, Dear! good Humour can prevail,
When Airs, and Flights, and Screams, and Scolding fail.
Beauties in vain their pretty eyes may roll;
Charms strike the Sight, but Merit wins the Soul.

From *The Rape of the Lock*
ALEXANDER POPE
(1688-1744)

A Day Off

I DON'T want
anything offensive
bothering me today
I have proclaimed
to my heart
that this will be
a clear clean
summer's day
no messing about
with dustbins
and other people's tragedies
no giving or taking
good advice
no guilt feelings about the past
just a sitting in the garden
watching-the-bees-work
sort of day.

URSULA LAIRD
(1919-   )

The Escape

I BELIEVE in the increasing of life; whatever
Leads to the seeing of small trifles,
Real, beautiful, is good; and an act never
Is worthier than in freeing spirit that stifles
Under ingratitude's weight, nor is anything done
Wiselier than the moving or breaking to sight
Of a thing hidden under by custom—revealed,
Fulfilled, used (sound-fashioned) any way out to
    delight:
Trefoil—hedge-sparrow—the stars on the edge at night.

IVOR GURNEY
(1890-1937)

The Trumpet

RISE up, rise up,
And, as the trumpet blowing
Chases the dreams of men,
As the dawn glowing
The stars that left unlit
The land and water,
Rise up and scatter
The dew that covers
The print of last night's lovers —
Scatter it, scatter it!

While you are listening
To the clear horn,
Forget, men, everything
On this earth new-born,
Except that it is lovelier
Than any mysteries.
Open your eyes to the air
That has washed the eyes of the stars
Through all the dewy night:
Up with the light,
To the old wars;
Arise, arise!

EDWARD THOMAS
(1878-1917)

You Must Break Through Old Thought

YOU must break through old thought
    As a seed through its rind,
You must be bound by naught
    Beyond your own young mind;

You must pierce old language
    As a fresh shoot pierces
Fallen leaves of an age
    That was, to one that is;

You must know your own need,
    You must nakedly dare,
To form a perfect deed,
    To fruit a spirit fair.

ELIZABETH DARYUSH
(1891-   )

Leap Before You Look

THE sense of danger must not disappear:
The way is certainly both short and steep,
However gradual it looks from here;
Look if you like, but you will have to leap.

Tough-minded men get mushy in their sleep
And break the by-laws any fool can keep;
It is not the convention but the fear
That has a tendency to disappear.

The worried efforts of the busy heap,
The dirt, the imprecision, and the beer
Produce a few smart wisecracks every year;
Laugh if you can, but you will have to leap.

The clothes that are considered right to wear
Will not be either sensible or cheap,
So long as we consent to live like sheep
And never mention those who disappear.

Much can be said for social savoir-faire,
But to rejoice when no one else is there
Is even harder than it is to weep;
No one is watching, but you have to leap.

A solitude ten thousand fathoms deep
Sustains the bed on which we lie, my dear:
Although I love you, you will have to leap:
Our dream of safety has to disappear.

W. H. AUDEN
(1907-1973)

They Are Playing a Game

THEY are playing a game. They are playing at not
playing a game. If I show them I see they are, I
shall break the rules and they will punish me.
I must play their game, of not seeing I see the game.

From *Knots 1*
R. D. LAING
(1927-   )

No Respect

I HAVE no respect for you
For you would not tell the truth about your grief
But laughed at it
When the first pang was past
And made it a thing of nothing.
You said
That what had been
Had never been
That what was
Was not:
You have a light mind
And a coward's soul.

STEVIE SMITH
(1905-1971)

Very very very many

VERY very very many
go through life without a penny
I have found this awfully true
in dealing with the well-to-do.

MICHAEL CARRIE
(1925-   )

The Signalman at Treblinka

SURELY, they said, he must have noticed something,
Despite the enveloping boughs, the hessian screen
That almost hid the wire perimeter.

Surely, they said, coming and going
To and from his cottage by the track
(Washed in blue to keep away the flies)
With its garden and the children's rabbit-hutch,
He must have wondered about the enveloping boughs,
The hessian screen, the wire perimeter.

But those are the commentators who always begin
Surely . . . or *One would have thought*
    . . . and have yet to learn
That the humble man can only avert his eyes:
His intervention would be farcical.
This man was humming a hit of '38,
Reliving a night in a dance-hall in Lodz,
As he swung the lever and under a rotten floor
Wires jerked, pulleys and rollers spun,
And the great locomotive crossed the points,
Hauling eighteen hundred human souls
(Little luggage, but such a burden of memories)
To a quiet siding where the pines sang
In a wind on which ashes were riding.

JOHN ADLARD
(1929-   )

Epitaph for Anton Schmidt

THE Schmidts obeyed, and marched on Poland,
And there an Anton Schmidt, Feldwebel,
Performed uncommon things, not safe
Nor glamorous, nor profitable.

Was the expression on his face
"Reposeful and humane good nature?"
Or did he look like any Schmidt,
Of slow and undisclosing feature?

I know he had unusual eyes,
Whose power no order might determine,
Not to mistake the men he saw,
As others did, for gods or vermin.

For five months, till his execution,
Aware that action has its dangers,
He helped the Jews to get away
— Another race at that, and strangers.

He never did mistake for bondage
The military job, the chances,
The limits; he did not submit
To the blackmail of his circumstances.

I see him in the Polish snow,
His muddy wrappings small protection,
Breathing the cold air of his freedom
And treading a distinct direction.

THOM GUNN
(1929-   )

Man, Take Your Gun

MAN, take your gun: and put to shame
earthquake and plague, the acts of God.
You maim the crazy and the lame.

Terror is their palsy, the knees
of men buckle for fear of man. You are the God whom
frenzy pleases.

You are the gas-man, and the flier
who drops his bomb; the man in tanks.
You wire mines and fear the fire.

And dig the hollow street with trenches
the gas-main and the sewer cross.
The stench of dead men makes you flinch.

But if the dying whimper, pain
pricks you like courage, like delight.
The vein sings to the cruel brain.

What are you, man, that gun in hand
with savagery and pity go,
and face to face with madness stand;

and acid-drenched and poison-sprayed
see flame run lovely like a wake
from raiders; and the burning lake
shake overhead? You are afraid.

The shadow flickers on the wall
like morse, like gun-shot. Terror walks
the tall roofs where the snipers hawk.
He stalks you, man. And, man, you fall.

JACOB BRONOWSKI
(1908-1974)

Vancouver Lights

ABOUT me the night   moonless   wimples the
   mountains
wraps ocean   land   air   and mounting
sucks at the stars   The city   throbbing below
webs the sable peninsula   The golden
strands overleap the seajet   by bridge and buoy
vault the shears of the inlet   climb the woods
toward me   falter   and halt   Across to the firefly
haze of a ship on the gulf's erased horizon
roll the lambent spokes of a lighthouse

Through the feckless years we have come to the time
when to look on this quilt of lamps is a troubling delight
Welling from Europe's bog   through Africa flowing
and Asia   drowning the lonely lumes on the oceans
tiding up over Halifax   now to this winking
outpost comes flooding the primal ink

On this mountain's brutish forehead with terror of space
I stir   of the changeless night and the stark ranges
of nothing   pulsing down from beyond and between
the fragile planets   We are a spark beleaguered
by darkness   this twinkle we make in a corner of
   emptiness
how shall we utter our fear that the black
   Experimentress
will never in the range of her microscope find it?   Our
   Phoebus
himself is a bubble that dries on Her slide   while the
   Nubian
wears for an evening's whim a necklace of nebulae

Yet we must speak   we the unique glowworms
Out of the waters and rocks of our little world
we conjured these flames   hooped these sparks
by our will   From blankness and cold we fashioned
   stars
to our size   and signalled Aldebaran
This must we say   whoever may be to hear us
if murk devour   and none weave again in gossamer:

                                    These rays were ours
we made and unmade them   Not the shudder of
    continents
doused us   the moon's passion   nor crash of comets
In the fathomless heat of our dwarfdom   our dream's
    combustion
we contrived the power   the blast that snuffed us
No one bound Prometheus   Himself he chained
and consumed his own bright liver   O stranger
Plutonian   descendant   or beast in the stretching
    night—
there was light

EARLE BIRNEY
(1904-   )

Money-Madness

MONEY is our madness, our vast collective madness.

And of course, if the multitude is mad
the individual carries his own grain of insanity around
    with him.
I doubt if any man living hands our pound note
    without a pang;
and a real tremor, if he hands out a ten-pound note.

We quail, money makes us quail.
It has got us down, we grovel before it in strange
    terror.
And no wonder, for money has a fearful cruel power
    among men.

But it is not money we are so terrified of,
It is the collective money-madness of mankind.
For mankind says with one voice: how much is he
    worth?
Has he no money? Then let him eat dirt, and go cold.

And if I have no money, they will give me a little
  bread
so I do not die,
but they will make me eat dirt with it.
I shall have to eat dirt, I shall have to eat dirt
if I have no money.

It is that that I am frightened of.
And that fear can become a delirium.
It is fear of my money-mad fellow-men.

We must have some money
to save us from eating dirt.

And this is all wrong.

Bread should be free,
shelter should be free,
fire should be free
to all and anybody, all over the world.

We must regain our sanity about money
before we start killing one another about it.
It's one or the other.

D. H. LAWRENCE
(1885-1930)

Peace the Great Meaning

PEACE the great meaning has not been defined.
When we say peace as a word, war
As a flare of fire leaps across our eyes.
We went to this school. Think war;
Cancel war, we were taught.
What is left is peace.
No, peace is not left, it is no cancelling;
The fierce and human peace is our deep power
Born to us of wish and responsibility.

MURIEL RUKEYSER

All Absolutes the Enemy

ALL Absolutes the enemy.
The part is greater than The Whole,
The voice that falters than The Soul.
Truth, Goodness, Beauty,
Embalm the rules, destroy the game,
Neatly snuff the candle flame.
Cradle-bound for Certainty,
We shun the light, grope for the breast,
Seek the safety of The Best.
All Absolutes the enemy.

JOHN GILMOUR
(1906-1986)

What is this Poetry?

"WHAT *is* this poetry," self whispered self,
But the endeavour, faithfully and well
As speech in language man-devised can,
To enshrine therein the inexpressible?

"See, now, the moon's declining crescent slim;
Thridding the stars in heaven she goes her way:
Yet doth she silver-tinge the virgin white
Of that clear cluster of jasmine on its spray.

"Ay, and my cheek her finger touched. I turned,
Through window scanned the seed-plot I could till,
And called a garden: and my heart stopped beating,
So marvellous its darkness, and so still. . . . "

Ours is that wine; that water clear and cool;
That very vineyard; and the troubled pool;
Wherewith to fill the thirsting spirit full.

Our utmost reach is what their content seems;
What mind surmises, and the heart esteems —
Ev'n though it be as transient as our dreams.

The true, the guileless, meaningful, and fair
Rest for their essence on our heed and care;
These are Earth's everything, Heaven's everywhere,
However small the commons we ourselves may
    share. . . .

From *Winged Chariot*
WALTER DE LA MARE
(1873-1956)

AUTHOR INDEX

LINE INDEX

From far, from eve and morning 119
From harmony, from heavenly harmony 160
From the private ease of Mother's womb 13

Gather ye rosebuds while ye may 119

Hark! the herald-Angels sing 180
Here lies one who never drew 128
He thanks whoever-she-is for her thoughtful 35
He thought he saw an Elephant 168
Hey nonny no 197
Hold thou the good: define it well 67
How many miles to Babylon 166
How round the world goes, and everything that's in it 109

I am the family face 8
I am watching them churn the last milk 129
I believe in the increasing of life; whatever 203
I came to him lightly 32
I can no longer ask how it feels 44
I don't want 202
I have no respect for you 205
I heard a bird at dawn 135
If all the world and love were young 199
If it could come to pass, and all kill all 181
If sadly thinking, with spirit sinking 197
If there be any God 99
I ne'er was struck before that hour 16
In melancholic fancy 156
In midst of woods or pleasant grove 136
In my craft or sullen art 49
In this little urn is laid 31
I remember God as an eccentric millionaire 93
I saw a fish pond all on fire 167
I saw a peacock with a fiery tail 166
Is it so small a thing 192
It is not growing like a tree 186
It isn't a very big cake 46
It is the Soul that sees; the outward eyes 18
I've held my tongue, dear John, quite long enough 28
I was an infant when my mother went 65
I went to the garden of love 63
I will live in Ringsend 200
I wish you for your birthday as you are 201

Know then thyself, presume not God to scan 8

Let me not to the marriage of true minds 187
Let others sing of knights and paladins 115
Like a small grey 129
Line upon line of cuttings 153

Man, take your gun: and put to shame 208
Man's life is well compared to a feast 103
Men heard this roar of parleying starlings, saw 75
Methinks 'tis pretty sport to hear a child 13
Money is our madness, our vast collective madness 210
Much have I travell'd in the realms of gold 159
Mute marriages 25
My heart is like a singing bird 16
My heart leaps up when I behold 186
My life closed twice before its close 73
My lord is the shepherd: his mark is upon me 89
My sweetest Lesbia, let us live and love 198

Naked I saw thee 196
Nervously face them, wish I had blushful 39
Nor happiness, nor majesty, nor fame 190
Now fades the last long streak of snow 30
Now Hoyle and Russell are the thing 88
Now I'm furnished for the flight 174

Oddments, as when 37
Oft in my laughing rhymes I name a gull 38
Oh! if to dance all Night, and dress all Day 202
Oh there is a place in Parnassus 95
O may I join the choir invisible 188
"O 'Melia, my dear, this does everything crown 27
One wan bird walks close to the mesh of the aviary 133
On the wide level of a mountain's head 107
Orpheus with his lute made trees 162
Our old wind crosses the tame border 115
Out in the dark over the snow 149

Past ruin'd Ilion Helen lives 116
Peace the great meaning has not been defined 211
People expect old men to die 31
Priests were the first deluders of mankind 53

Rich as the stars and poor as a beggar 15
Rise up, rise up 203

Said Zwingli to Muntzer 84
Say it were true that thou outliv'st us all 130
Say the soft bird's name, but do not be surprised 141
Science! thou fair effusive ray 60
Setting mine hour-glass for a witness by 104
She rose to his requirement, dropped 39
Should you revisit us 90
Seamen three! What men be ye 169
Sleep, Death's ally, oblivion of tears 35
Some people are flower lovers 142
Songs of thankfulness and praise 179